T0285324

PENTECOST AT TEPEYAC?

PENTECOST AT TEPEYAC?

Pneumatologies from the People

ORLANDO O. ESPÍN

ORBIS BOOKS
Maryknoll, New York 10545

Founded in 1970, Orbis Books endeavors to publish works that enlighten the mind, nourish the spirit, and challenge the conscience. The publishing arm of the Maryknoll Fathers and Brothers, Orbis seeks to explore the global dimensions of the Christian faith and mission, to invite dialogue with diverse cultures and religious traditions, and to serve the cause of reconciliation and peace. The books published reflect the views of their authors and do not represent the official position of the Maryknoll Society. To learn more about Maryknoll and Orbis Books, please visit our website at www.orbisbooks.com

Copyright © 2024 by Orlando O Espín

Published by Orbis Books, Box 302, Maryknoll, NY 10545-0302.

All rights reserved.

No part of this publication may be reproduced or transmitted in any form or by any means, electronic or mechanical, including photocopying, recording, or any information storage or retrieval system, without prior permission in writing from the publisher.

Queries regarding rights and permissions should be addressed to: Orbis Books, P.O. Box 302, Maryknoll, NY 10545-0302.

Manufactured in the United States of America

Library of Congress Cataloging-in-Publication Data

Names: Espín, Orlando O., author.
Title: Pentecost at Tepeyac? : pneumatologies from the people / Orlando O. Espín.
Description: Maryknoll, NY : Orbis Books, [2024] | Includes bibliographical references and index. | Summary: "A study of the cult of Our Lady of Guadalupe—a form of Marian devotion, or a popular expression of pneumatology?"— Provided by publisher.
Identifiers: LCCN 2023033907 (print) | LCCN 2023033908 (ebook) | ISBN 9781626985605 | ISBN 9798888660188 (epub)
Subjects: LCSH: Guadalupe, Our Lady of—Cult. | Guadalupe, Our Lady of—History. | Holy Spirit.
Classification: LCC BT660.G8 E85 2024 (print) | LCC BT660.G8 (ebook) | DDC 232.91/7097253—dc23/eng/20230915
LC record available at https://lccn.loc.gov/2023033907
LC ebook record available at https://lccn.loc.gov/2023033908

Para Ricardo, compañero y amigo.
Porque nunca me alcanzará la vida para agradecerle la vida.

Para

Alfonso García Rubio, maestro

y

Robert W. McElroy, obispo.

A la memoria de mi padre y mi madre, de Nery y Mario,
de Lourdes y Eduardo,
doña Estela, doña Antonia.
John J. Nevins, Ada M. Isasi-Díaz,
Virgilio Elizondo, Otto Maduro y Edgard Beltrán.

Y para

Laura y Rodolfo. Ramiro. Germán. Martha R. Carolina.
Édgar y Chris, Ana Laura y Marimar,
Fernanda y Joel, Karolina y Eduardo.
Luna Selene y Tía Licha.
May y Chemo. Marian, Damián y Máriko.
Isabel y Arturo. Héctor y Ana.
Delsy y Daniel. Marisol y David. Mariela.
Ramón y Jacqueline. Isara y José. Jéssica y Tito.
Orlando y Leslie. Esteban.
Amelia, Alejandro, Isabella y Victoria.

Mary C. Doak	Justo L. González
Arturo J. Bañuelas	Víctor Carmona
Gustavo Gutiérrez	Peter A. Mena
Luis Rivera Pagán	Roberto S. Goizueta
Raúl Fornet-Betancourt	Carmen Nanko-Fernández
John D. Gillespie	Paloma Olivares G.
Peter C. Phan	Jonathan Y. Tan
Eliezer y María L. Valentín	Jane C. Redmont
Jean-Pierre Ruiz	Bahar Davary
Sixto J. García	Miguel H. Díaz
Rubén Rosario R.	Silvia Muñoz

Fides populi quaerens intellectum ad transformationem mundi.

God chose the foolish of the world to shame the wise.
God chose the lowly and despised of the world,
those who count for nothing,
to reduce to nothing those who are something.

I Corinthians 1:27–29

We cannot live in a world that is not our own,
in a world that is interpreted for us by others.
Part of the dare is to take back our own listening,
to use our own voice, to see our own light.

Hildegard of Bingen

Let us pray to God that we may be free of "God."

Meister Eckhart

The only true representation is one
that also represents its distance from the truth.

Giorgio Agamben

CONTENTS

Introduction

For many years I have been discussing a number of questions regarding the defining roles of culture and cultural symbols, as well as the roles played by contexts of conquest and dominance, in the formation and development of Latinoax[1] popular

---

[1] In this book, breaking with my own past usage, I choose to employ the neologism *Latinoax* instead of other parallel terms, because *Latinoax* allows pronunciation and recognition by most of us (i.e., by Latinoax generations, families, communities, and persons), while also and importantly being gender inclusive, non-binary, and non-conforming—*and* because it avoids the possibly surreptitious self-colonization conveyed by "Latinx" in the name of "equality" and "inclusiveness." Being "equal to" or "fitting in" should by defined by us, in *our* terms. Furthermore, we very much need to understand "us" without replicating imported prejudices, assumptions, or marginalizations. The people in our communities are "us" as much as (more than!) our scholars, and as much as those of any one generation. *Latinoax* is a noun, singular and plural, and also an adjective, while *latinamente* is the corresponding adverb. These terms refer *only* to United States populations of Latin American ancestry; therefore, "Latinoax" is *not* synonymous with "Latin American." The still frequent use of "Hispanic" as preferred term over "Latinoax" is problematic for two reasons: 1. It assumes that the way to identify our communities is through the conqueror/colonizer, thereby again surreptitiously establishing the Eurocentric as the best identity-defining category or grantor of our identity; and 2. It hides the continued and clear presence and cultural contributions among Latinoax of Latin America's

Catholicism. The consequences for theology (and not just for Latinoax theology) are too serious to ignore or downplay.

In the introduction to my *The Faith of the People*[2] I hinted at some of the pneumatological possibilities that could be unveiled in a careful cultural and theological study of some supposedly Marian symbols. The present (intentionally brief) book continues those earlier reflections, but has no pretension of concluding them. Years of thoughtful conversations with many families, scholars, students, and others are reflected in these pages.

I think it important, however, to begin by offering the reader the personal context that made me wonder about the pneuma-

---

Native peoples and of the Native peoples of the US southwest, as well as the presence and important contributions of millions of African slaves and their descendants. The post-independence histories of the Latin American peoples have also made an impact on today's Latinoax, their cultural identities, and their communal histories. Nevertheless, "Hispanic" is an appropriate adjective when referring to those persons of only Iberian ancestry, or explicitly to those elements of Latinoax cultures and communities that are clearly and unambiguously Iberian. There are serious consequences for theology resulting from the present—and rapidly increasing—Latinoax demographic and cultural presence in US society and the US Catholic Church (e.g., Latinoax are already nearly half of all US Catholics, and this fact *doctrinally* disrupts the naïve assumption that the "Church" is only or mainly coextensive with the Eurocentric). The US Catholic Church (especially its institutions, bishops, and clergy) sooner than later must confront its assumed cultural Eurocentrism, and its evident racial (white-privileging) and ethnic prejudices—because these contradict the necessary and non-negotiable doctrinal claim that *the Church is the People of God.*

    [2] Orlando Espín, *The Faith of the People: Theological Reflections on Popular Catholicism* (Maryknoll, NY: Orbis, 1997), esp. 6–10.

tological possibilities in some apparently Marian devotional expressions—and their potential theological consequences.

I was born in Cuba and in very early adolescence arrived in the US. I grew up surrounded by Marian devotions: the *Virgen de la Caridad del Cobre* (Our Lady of Charity, patroness of Cuba, whose basilica is in the town of El Cobre in eastern Cuba), the *Virgen de Fátima*, the *Virgen de Belén*. Obviously, family history determined which Marian devotional practices were to be important for us. But in each and every one of these devotions it was also clear that the focus was Mary, the mother of Jesus.[3] She was held up as the first disciple of her son, as a model of Christian living, and as the one to plead with her Son on our behalf. No other human ever had or will have the privilege of giving birth to the Christ. But there was more that was much more central to our being a Catholic family: standing up for the marginalized was a non-negotiable, as were daily Eucharist, annual Ignatian retreats, and serious religious education—much of it thanks to the Jesuits who had educated my grandfather and my father in Cuba and with whom my father remained close, which also led to both my brother and me studying in Havana's and Miami's Jesuit schools. Life later

---

[3] As far as I know, no one in my family has been or is a member of the Lukumí religion ("Santería"), frequent in Cuba and among Cuban Americans. Hence, I did not grow up believing that the *Virgen de la Caridad* stands for *Oshún*, the Yoruba *orisha*, although I have always known that many believe so, because it is culturally impossible to be Cuban and not be touched by, or aware of, the Lukumí religion. I am unquestionably respectful of the Lukumí and their religious traditions, and my not participating in them cannot be interpreted to mean disparagement.

brought me to the Dominican Republic (and thus to the *Virgen de la Altagracia* and the *Virgen de la Merced*) and to Brazil (and to *Nossa Senhora Aparecida*).

Throughout my life, until 1991, I lived mostly in an Antillean, Atlantic world. That year I moved to San Diego, on the US-Mexico border, and became a member of the theology faculty at the University of San Diego. I have remained on this border, even after retirement three decades later. Here I met the *Virgen de Guadalupe*, through the devotional expressions of both Mexicans and Mexican Americans. I have since married into a Mexican family, with members on both sides of the imaginary line that distinguishes, but certainly cannot separate, the two nations of Mexico and the United States.

I knew of Guadalupe before coming to San Diego, of course, but I had never witnessed the depth of devotion to her until I came to live among her devotees. For me, as a Cuban American, the devotional intensity I saw among Guadalupe's Mexican and Mexican American devotees appeared to be extreme—bordering, or so I first thought, on the idolatrous. How could anyone be a Catholic Christian and relate to Mary in ways reserved only for God? By 1991, I had already spent over a decade observing and studying popular Catholicism, but this Mexican devotion seemed too much! Until one day, three years after my arrival in San Diego, during Guadalupe's December celebrations at (and on the streets around) Our Lady of Angels parish church, in one of the most Mexican neighborhoods of San Diego, one of the grandmothers who belonged to the *Guadalupanas* women's group said to me, very proudly, *"Vea, maestro, ¡Dios se viste de mujer!"* ("Look, teacher,

God dresses up as a woman!"). At that moment, the proverbial lightbulb lit up, and I started wondering if instead of an overly exaggerated Marian devotion I had not been witnessing something else, very far from the idolatrous.

That moment led me to the pneumatological questions I first raised in *The Faith of the People*, and in a few later texts.[4] I still cannot conclude my search for understanding, although this book will offer the reader an idea of where these many years of participant observation, conversations, study, and reflection have brought me. This intellectual journey is not finished.

This brief volume seeks to lead us to another possible understanding of the Guadalupe devotion. It also wants to recognize the limits and serious blind spots of many theological approaches and doctrinal assumptions that we have inherited from Eurocentric intellectual and religious traditions whose attempts at understanding the non-Eurocentric are conducted, at best, through a set of *lentes borrosos*,[5] thereby leading to conclusions that are often insufficient, biased, or wrong. Guadalupe led me to question the need and possibility of another pneumatology—one that may lead to the subversion of hegemonies in this world. Guadalupe, I learned, subverts the assumed.

Before that 1994 Guadalupe procession in San Diego's *Barrio Logan*, I thought I understood. But I clearly had not.

I will reflect here, however briefly, on human culture and power asymmetries, because all theology is human, cultural,

---

[4] For example, Orlando Espín, "Mary in Latino/a Catholicism: Four Types of Devotion," *New Theology Review* 23, no. 3 (2010): 16–25.

[5] Lentes borrosos = "blurred lenses."

expressed within the bounds of language, and inescapably crafted within the contexts of societies' asymmetric power struggles. In these pages we will study the possibilities and ways of *one* specific symbol that expresses faith in the Holy Spirit in manners both Catholic and Latinoax, but not Hellenic or Eurocentric.[6] I will also reflect on the potential consequences of the implied pneumatology.

All pneumatologies, without exception, are limited and transient, perspectival, contextual and contextualized, stammering to understand and express the One who is beyond all human understanding or expression—and this attempt does not pretend to be otherwise. Think of these pages as "notes toward," or "an outline for," an inclusive dialogue on pneumatology, directly engaging culture, contexts, and social/ecclesial power asymmetries; but still a dialogue on pneumatology that I hope will point to the transformation of this world according to the core of Jesus' preaching.

For me it is important that by way of reasoned arguments, connections to broader issues, bibliographical references, and more, these pages elicit, invite, and suggest further thoughts, conversations, and life commitments. What I (or any other author) might propose is not and cannot be the definitive word on any aspect or consequence of pneumatology or of any other theological discipline. A contribution is only a contribution.

This is a volume within "western Catholic" theology.[7]

---

[6] And I should also specify: in manners not androcentric, "white," heteronormative, or hegemonic.

[7] See Orlando Espín, *Idol and Grace: On Traditioning and Subversive Hope* (Maryknoll, NY: Orbis, 2014), 13–38. There I explain that western Catholicism, in my understanding—and demonstrably in

Having that acknowledged as the theological location of this book, we must also acknowledge the frequent temptation of western Catholic theologians to assume that there is *one* "mainstream," assumed by many to be the Eurocentric (androcentric or feminist) manner or method of doing theology. What many theologians do not notice, and thus do not acknowledge, is that what most regard as the "mainstream" seems too conveniently coextensive with the theological assumptions and methods of the culturally and socially dominant (i.e., white, Eurocentric, male, heterosexual—and also, too often, white feminist).

---

fact—is a *perspective* within which (historically speaking) most western Christians have understood and "traditioned," and still understand, tradition and live their faith. Western Catholicism is a way of "doing," living, and praying Christianity, and only secondarily a way of "doctrinifying" or explaining it. These are the reasons why I am convinced that western Catholicism cannot be reduced to a single denomination or a single ecclesial communion. I prefer to include under the label "western Catholic" the Roman Catholic, Anglican/Episcopal, Old Catholic, and (most of the) Lutheran and Methodist ecclesial communions (as long as by "communions" we do not understand "ecclesiastical institutions" or denominations). Most of today's western Catholics, according to this broader meaning of the expression, are in countries of the so-called "Third [or Two-Thirds] World." Many are also members of "minoritized" communities in the countries of the so-called "First [or One-Third] World." Consequently, "western Catholicism" is not coextensive with or defined by the dominant (white, male or female, heterosexual, Eurocentric), despite their pretensions and explanations, because "western Catholicism" (in basic western Catholic ecclesiology) *is the People*—the majority of whom are demonstrably marginalized, dismissed, and/or abused by the dominant, sometimes with the acquiescence of the institutions of religion.

Many theologians do not notice.[8] And consequently, the absence of elements of the expected dominant theologies' "mainstream" in the theological works of the "unimportant" tends to be viewed (by those "mainstream" theologians) as if there were something "important" missing, or as if this were a methodological flaw. The present volume does not claim a location within that self-appointed "mainstream." Latinoax theology does not imitate, and does not need to imitate, what the socio-culturally dominant have declared as "necessary" or "expected" by conveniently setting themselves as the best standard of scholarly quality or methodological rigor. Engagement and dialogue cannot be construed (ethically and/or academically) as attempts at imitation or colonization. If theology is *fides quaerens intellectum ad transformationem mundi*,[9] then the expected methodologies cannot naïvely reproduce and maintain the current power asymmetries in the world.[10] The

----

[8] This also implies that many western Catholic theologians forget—intentionally or not—the foundational insight undergirding the claim that the Church is and needs to always be "catholic," or it stops being the Church. This insight is not about widespread geographic presence but, rather, emphatically about openness to and inclusion of all, not as guests but as equal partners with equal rights and obligations in the same community.

[9] "Faith in search of understanding for the transformation of the world." I am convinced that Anselm of Canterbury would have agreed with this expanded paraphrase.

[10] The reader might benefit from engaging Antonio Gramsci's notions of "cultural hegemony" and of "intellectual." See Antonio Gramsci, *Concepção Dialética da Historia* [trans. of *Il materialismo storico e la filosofia di Benedetto Croce*] (Rio de Janeiro: Ed. Civilização Brasileira, 1981); Gramsci, *Os Intelectuais e a Organização da Cultura*

transformation of the world is the goal—because that is the core of Jesus' message of the dawning Reign of God.

Because I am a Latinoax Christian in the western Catholic tradition, I have written this book as a theological construct grounded in, from, and on Latinoax communities; but it is not just for or about Latinoax.

Readers familiar with my previous work and publications will notice that I bring up in the following pages insights and thoughts that I have discussed elsewhere before. This proved inevitable in this intentionally brief volume. The point of these pages is not repetition but the elaboration of one insight I shared in *The Faith of the People*, and for that purpose I employ contributions I made via some earlier work.

* * *

The several quotations with which I open this book have been and remain important signposts in my theological work and have guided this particular reflection. Each of them merits the reader's consideration and reflection.

I again thank those to whom I have dedicated this book. They have contributed to my life and thought over many years.[11] I am particularly grateful to the Mexican and Mexican American extended families who have, over the years, shared their reflections on their faith and lives with me; they too

---

[trans. of *Gli intelletuali e l'organizzazione della cultura*] (Rio de Janeiro: Ed. Civilização Brasileira, 1979); and indispensably, Luciano Gruppi, *O Conceito de Hegemonia em Gramsci* (Rio de Janeiro: Ed. Graal, 1980).

[11] See also the Acknowledgments at the end of this volume.

have been indispensable to this volume. My thanks also to Prof. Jean-Pierre Ruiz of St. John's University in New York for suggesting this book's apt title.

Orlando O. Espín
San Diego, CA

1

Challenges and Contexts
of All Pneumatologies

The First Important Issue in Pneumatology

If I were to translate literally the common Spanish expression *por si las moscas*, it would be rendered in English as "for if the flies." This translation, however, would entirely miss the meaning and idiomatic use of the phrase. It would be a bad translation.[1] Knowing the meaning of words does not mean one knows the language and its historical and cultural development, or the language's idiomatic use of words and expressions, or the language's intent in the specific or general use of words.

The same must be said of doctrines and symbols. We might know the words employed by doctrinal statements, but we cannot assume that because we know the meaning of terms, we fully or truly understand their meaning or intent, especially the meaning or intent of words or symbols others crafted and employed in cultural, socioeconomic, linguistic, and historical contexts very different from our own.[2]

---

[1] The phrase is used in everyday Spanish to mean "just in case."

[2] We cannot say or believe that we understand the history of

The Council of Nicaea's creed (325 CE), as expanded by
the Council of Constantinople (381 CE), says: "We believe in
the Holy Spirit, the Lord, the Giver of life, who proceeds from
the Father, who with the Father and the Son is worshipped
and glorified, and who spoke through the prophets." There has
been some discussion regarding the exact origin of these creedal
phrases, which today form part of the Nicene-Constantinop-
olitan Creed's pneumatological section, although it is known
that anti-Pneumatomachian[3] arguments provided the immediate context and motive. Regardless of these phrases' origin,
this creed—which has included these phrases since the patristic
period—is accepted as orthodox expression of their faith by

---

languages (anyone else's as well as our own) if we dismiss the ever-
changing meaning of many terms, uses, and expressions, and the
creation of new ones. Every language is inescapably situated and
evolving. Translations cannot avoid being, at best, approximations—
and at worst, betrayals. Centuries (indeed, millennia) do not pass
without consequences for sociocultural formations ("historical blocs"
in Gramscian terms) and thus for languages, understandings, and
perspectives from and through which generations assume they are able
to understand across time.

    [3] The Pneumatomachians (also but inaccurately called
Macedonians, after a deposed mid-fourth century patriarch of
Constantinople) were condemned by the Council of Constantinople
of 381 CE. They seem to have been a diverse group of Arian and non-
Arian theologians who denied the divinity (but not the existence)
of the Holy Spirit. Their more frequent argument ran parallel to
the Arian argument denying the divinity of the Son. See Rosemary
P. Carbine, "Pneumatomachians," in *An Introductory Dictionary of
Theology and Religious Studies*, ed. Orlando Espín and J. Nickoloff
(Collegeville, MN: Liturgical Press, 2007), 1053.

the vast majority of Christians.[4] It is important to note that the addition of the *Filioque* ("... and the Son") by western Christianity during the sixth century apparently seemed the only way to doctrinally avoid an Arian interpretation of the Latin verb *procedere*, which was the most frequent translation (in the West) of the creed's Greek *ekporeuomai*.[5]

No one questions that these creedal expressions were crafted by specific humans, in specific cultural and historical contexts, for specific purposes. These creedal statements have throughout Christian history been "received" by equally specific humans, in specific and numerous cultural and historical contexts, for purposes arguably unaware of the Pneumatomachians, of their heresy, and of their ancient "orthodox" opponents. In other words, the creedal statements were contextualized in their origin and remain contextualized in their historically varied and culturally diverse receptions.[6] But just as the Latin West considered necessary the addition

---

[4] The Roman Catholic, Anglican, Old Catholic, and Orthodox Communions, as well as many "mainline" Protestants (e.g., the churches of the Lutheran World Federation) accept this ancient creed as orthodox expression of their faith.

[5] See the joint "Agreed Statement" of the official North American Orthodox-Catholic Consultation, *The Filioque: A Church-Dividing Issue?* (Washington, DC: United States Conference of Catholic Bishops, 2003).

[6] See Stanley M. Burgess, *The Holy Spirit: Ancient Christian Traditions* (Peabody, MA: Hendrickson, 1990). Burgess continued his study of the development of pneumatological doctrines in a second volume on eastern Christian traditions and in a third volume on medieval and early modern (Catholic and Reformation) mostly Eurocentric traditions.

of the *Filioque* to the original Greek text in order to maintain the intended creedal meaning, we must admit that *for the
same reason* the intended creedal meanings regarding the Holy
Spirit must also be "expressible" in non-Greek, non-Latin, non-
Mediterranean, non-Eurocentric, non-dominant, non-white,
non-gender-normative, and historically diverse contexts. This
is important, indeed inescapable.

It is clear to me that the first crucial issue when discussing
pneumatology is the need to acknowledge explicitly that what
we say in and through one cultural, symbolic, linguistic, and
socioeconomic context might not mean or allow for the same
meaning when expressed in a different cultural, symbolic,
linguistic, or socioeconomic context. It is also inescapably
evident that no context can pretend that any of its expressions
and meanings exhausts or expresses all that could be expressed
or meant. In fact, to convey the same meaning might require,
by unavoidable cultural and historical re-contextualizing,
seemingly different (or even apparently opposing) means of
expression which will, in turn, probably unveil new or different
depths or dimensions of and in the meaning. "Translation," in
the original meaning of the term, "to carry over," is inescapable.

Pneumatology, as a theological discipline, is manifestly
cultural. It cannot be otherwise because humans craft theology,
and all things crafted by humans are cultural, without exception. When the term "pneumatology" is used as a "gathering
label" to group the Christian doctrines and doctrinal reflections regarding the Holy Spirit, pneumatology is also evidently
and inescapably cultural. In fact, all doctrinal statements are
cultural constructs, and cannot be otherwise—even those
which ecclesial communities regard as "revealed" by God—

because even revelation is inescapably cultural. Revelation is not a one-way pronouncement (or multiple pronouncements) from God. Revelation, in order to be heard and understood as such, requires listeners—and these listeners are inescapably contextualized in their respective cultures, social power asymmetries, and other contextual realities. Hence, what the listeners understand and name has been and will be understood and named from within their cultural and historical contexts.[7] God is certainly not limited by culture, but humans are, as are all human understandings (and misunderstandings) of what humans believe God has revealed.

Consequently, all doctrinal statements are cultural, regardless of their claimed normative authority, and regardless of our awareness of, or blindness to, the reality and limiting impact of cultural contexts.[8] All understandings (and misunderstandings)

---

[7] It is of vital importance that we recall that the definitive revelation of God's will and being *is* Jesus of Nazareth, as we will now proceed to discuss in the text. The Council of Chalcedon's (451 CE) affirmations regarding Jesus cannot be ignored ("human like us in all things, except for sin" [Denzinger-Hünermann, *Enchiridion Symbolorum*, 301–302]). Jesus's words are important because they are *his*, and not the other way around.

[8] Much of what follows here has been the focus of my theological work over many years. I have often discussed culture, power asymmetries, symbols, the ineffability of the Mystery we call God, etc., as inescapable contexts of theology and religion, especially of "popular" Catholicism, and of the *sensus fidelium*, revelation, and traditioning. Because of their contextualizing inescapability, I here return again to these issues. More extensive reflections can be found in Orlando Espín, *The Faith of the People: Theological Reflections on Popular Catholicism* (Maryknoll, NY: Orbis, 1997); Espín, *Grace and*

of doctrines are the unavoidable result of "carrying over" (i.e., "translating") prior insights, experiences, and understandings into new contexts.

The Contextualized Reality of All Doctrines About God

All Christian doctrines are human claims. There is no way to escape this fact. Their being "true" or not is also a human claim regarding doctrines, as much as the claim that (some) doctrines are part of "revelation."

For Christians, Jesus of Nazareth is not just the revealer. He *is* the revelation of God. This too is a human claim, but it is the most foundational of all claims made by Christianity. Everything in Christianity stands or falls on what and who and whether Jesus *is*. And if Jesus of Nazareth is the revelation of God, then revelation is inescapably cultural—because, as truly human,[9] Jesus was in and of a culture, and therefore understood, lived, and spoke in and through it. Furthermore, all

---

Humanness: Theological Reflections Because of Culture (Maryknoll, NY: Orbis, 2007); Espín, *Idol and Grace: On Traditioning and Subversive Hope* (Maryknoll, NY: Orbis, 2014); and also in a number of articles I have published over the years in the *Journal of Hispanic/ Latino Theology* (now the *Journal of Hispanic/Latinoax Theology*) and in chapters within collective volumes. Consequently, a reader familiar with my work will recognize in what follows reflections that, in one way or another, I have engaged before.

[9] Again, we must recall the Council of Chalcedon's affirmation regarding Jesus, "human like us in all things, except for sin." We must remember (also in reference to Jesus) that no human is human without culture.

understandings regarding Jesus are by humans who were and are in and of their respective cultures.

I start this pneumatological reflection, therefore, by acknowledging that "claim making" is unavoidable in the religion we call Christianity and in its theologies. Claim making is as unavoidable as needing to start here by understanding that *the making of claims is always a cultural construct* that happens in time and in history (which are not coextensive).

Cultures

Societies are shaped by cultures, and vice versa. All human thinking and thoughts, human languages and symbols, all human evidence and "established facts," what humans claim "is there" and what humans claim "is not," what humans accept as "reason" and "reasonable," what is regarded as "good" or as "bad," whom humans regard as "human" and "equal," and whom humans do not, and a very long etcetera—*all* are cultural constructs.

This book and every thought in it are cultural creations because culture is a context we cannot avoid or even imagine escaping, because there is no human and nothing human without culture.

We are only and always in culture. Culture itself is always within time and transience—which necessarily means that all cultures change and pass.

To define culture is in itself a cultural act. The act of defining culture, furthermore, is neither ethically innocent nor interest-neutral. This is especially so when we attempt to define or understand the culture of another: we must be very aware that such act occurs from, within, and because of our own culture. *We* decide to define or understand another's culture, for *our* purposes and interests; but the other is in no way bound (by that other's culture) to be as we define or understand them. To think otherwise is certainly naïve, and just as certainly a display of cultural hubris. The other is also probably understanding and defining our culture for the other's cultural purposes and interests, and we do not feel obligated to accept or be like the other's understanding or definition of us. The long and unfortunate human history of conquests, slaveries, and colonizations is a clear though horrifying example of cultural universes needing to define and understand each other for each side's purposes and interests. Sometimes the survival of a people has rested on this dynamic.[10]

I have elsewhere[11] described "culture" as the historically and ecologically possible means and ways through which a people construct and unveil themselves (to themselves, and only secondarily to others) as meaningfully human, constructing their meaning of "human" in this same process. The values, meanings, and goals of cultures, which define the human communities that construct them, have a decisive impact on the social organization of the contextual-material universes that these communities affirm as their own because

---

[10] See Ernesto Laclau, *On Populist Reason* (New York: Verso, 2007), 65–172.

[11] See Espín, *Idol and Grace*, 44–46. Consider also Néstor Medina, "Toward Understanding the Contextual Theo-Ethical Anthropology of Orlando Espín," in *T&T Clark Handbook of Theological Anthropology*, ed. Mary Ann Hinsdale and Stephen Okey (London: Bloomsbury/T&T Clark, 2021), 305–316.

they *are in them*. Even the most marginalized cultures are still meaningful vehicles of meaningful interpretations of life and reality for the communities that construct and claim them.[12] It is within, and from within, this meaningfulness that human communities create and speak their logic, their perspectives, their sense of life, and their meanings, and engage in their quest for what they (again, culturally) regard as truth. It is within and from within this meaningfulness too that human communities universalize their interpretive universes.[13]

---

[12] See James C. Scott, *Weapons of the Weak: Everyday Forms of Peasant Resistance* (New Haven: Yale University Press, 1987) and Scott, *Domination and the Arts of Resistance: Hidden Transcripts* (New Haven: Yale University Press, 1990).

[13] On culture, see Rodolfo Kusch, *Obras completas*, vols.1–3 (Buenos Aires: Editorial Fundación Ross, 2000), [Rodolfo Kusch was one of Latin America's great theorists of culture]; Alexis Jardines, *El cuerpo y lo otro. Introducción a una teoría general de la cultura* (Havana: Ed. de Ciencias Sociales, 2004); Boaventura de Souza Santos, *Una epistemología del sur* (Buenos Aires: Siglo XXI, 2009); Homi K. Bhabha, *The Location of Culture* (London: Routledge, 2004); David Sobrevilla, ed., *Filosofía de la cultura* (Madrid: Trotta, 1998); Bradd Shore, *Culture in Mind: Cognition, Culture, and the Problem of Meaning* (New York: Oxford University Press, 1996); George Yúdice, *The Expediency of Culture: Uses of Culture in the Global Era* (Durham: Duke University Press, 2003); Pierre Bourdieu, *Acts of Resistance: Against the Tyranny of the Market* (New York: New Press, 1998); Bourdieu, *Language and Symbolic Power* (Cambridge, MA: Harvard University Press, 1991); Peter L. Berger and Thomas Luckmann, *The Social Construction of Reality* (New York: Doubleday, 1966); and Orlando Espín, "Culture," in *Introductory Dictionary of Theology and Religious Studies*, 302.

Culture, therefore, has primarily to do with the construction of meaningfulness and humanness, the latter two terms being mutually imbricating. In other words, *we are human because we have constructed the meaningfulness of our being human.* Hence, without or outside of culture we would not be human or meaningful to ourselves, individually or collectively.

Cultures are human creations; and all that shapes humanness is in culture. This necessarily implies that conflict and power asymmetries are also part of culture, and shapers thereof.

As Pierre Bourdieu, Antonio Gramsci, Raúl Fornet-Betancourt, Rodolfo Kusch, Judith Butler, and others have demonstrated,[14] in any historical period the shape of any society—as well as the shape of any society's culture—is a reflection of the society's internal asymmetries. These asymmetries in turn reflect the social struggles for the power to establish *the* meaning and purpose of (socially constructed) reality, according to the historical period's victors in that social struggle. In other words, the constructed meaningfulness of our being human (i.e., our culture) is always conflictual, asymmetrical, and shaped through the exercise of dominant power—which necessarily implies the parallel exercise of the power to marginalize the non-dominant, non-victorious others. But dominant power is never definitively established in any culture. Instead, it will always be fought over, although not all who struggle share the same weapons. Symbolic weapons,

---

[14] See the immediately preceding and following notes for bibliographic references.

needless to say, are among the most powerful (and convincing) in the arsenals of social conflict.[15] Later in this volume we

---

[15] Religious doctrines, rituals, and devotional symbols can be among these symbolic weapons. Evidently, the importance of one or another, and their "official" interpretations (which are ideologically assumed to be "best"), will be produced and "established" according to the interests of the beneficiaries of society's hegemonic power asymmetries. However, this does not mean that the marginalized by society (i.e., the subaltern, in Gramscian terms) are left without their own symbolic weapons. In other words, those made invisible by and to society's dominant also produce *their* doctrines, rituals, devotional symbols, and interpretations which *they* hold as "best." We shall see how re-interpretation, "carrying over," re-contextualization, and shared performance can and do open public subversive spaces for those made invisible or marginalized. Meanwhile, see de Souza Santos, *Una epistemología del sur*, as well as Scott, *Weapons of the Weak* and Scott, *Domination and the Arts of Resistance*. The influence of Gramsci's thought on mine is evident here. See Antonio Gramsci, *Literatura e vida nacional* (Mexico City: Juan Pablos, 1998); Gramsci, *Concepção dialética da história* (Rio de Janeiro: Civilização Brasileira, 1955); Gramsci, *Cadernos do cárcere* (Rio de Janeiro: Civilização Brasileira, 2022); Gramsci, *Cartas do cárcere* (Rio de Janeiro: Civilização Brasileira, 2005); and Gramsci, *Os intelectuais e a organização da cultura* [trans. of *Gli intellettuali e l'organizzazione della cultura*] (Rio de Janeiro: Civilização Brasileira, 1979). See also Luciano Gruppi, *O conceito de hegemonia em Gramsci* (Rio de Janeiro: Ed. Graal, 1980); Hugues Portelli, *Gramsci et le bloc historique* (Paris: Presses Universitaires de France, 1972); and Kate A. Crehan, *Gramsci, Culture and Anthropology* (Berkeley: University of California Press, 2002). The idea of hegemony here, of course, is Gramsci's, but accompanied by my reading of Ernesto Laclau. By or on the latter, See Laclau, *On Populist Reason*; Ernesto Laclau and Chantal Mouffe, *Hegemony and Socialist Strategy*, 2nd ed.

will discuss one specific case of re-interpretation—and transformation (i.e., "carrying over")—by the vanquished, of their meaning for, and relationship with, a symbol originally imposed by the dominant. Translation[16] is unavoidable in order to make sense.

We need to acknowledge explicitly that all cultures, therefore, act as mirrors of their power asymmetries regarding race and ethnicity, "peoplehood," nationality, and citizenship, gender, gender identity, and sexual orientation, employment and social class, access to knowledge and education, and access to (quantity, quality, and type of) food and land, as well as to health care and housing, to security and safety, and to a long list of etceteras.

Referring all of the above to the Christian religion, it becomes evident that whoever has the power to make the religion's claims, and to socially (and ecclesially) establish them by further claiming that they are from God, controls the most powerful symbolic weapon in the religion, and in the societies and cultures that have been shaped by it. Doctrines, needless to add, are also the result of a religion's internal struggles for the hegemonic exercise of symbolic dominant power.[17]

(London: Verso, 2001); and Simon Critchley and Oliver Marchart, eds., *Laclau: A Critical Reader* (London: Routledge, 2004). I have never been able to explain why the influential philosopher Giorgio Agamben has so thoroughly ignored Gramsci's and Laclau's social analyses and categories.

[16] I remind the reader that the original meaning of "translation" is "carrying over."

[17] Recognition of the role(s) of conflict and of hegemonic symbolic power (especially the roles of symbol for and within hegemony) helps

This does not logically require the historically untenable conclusion that all doctrinal claims are mere fabrications for the political manipulation of the simple—or that there always is some sort of evil intent in establishing doctrines. But it does logically require that we acknowledge that doctrines are not socially, culturally, or hegemonically innocent. Because doctrines are human claims, they too bear the (humanizing and dehumanizing) realities of humanness, including the struggles for dominance, thereby including and displaying what Christianity calls "sin."

Just as dominant power is never definitively established in any culture or society but is constantly fought over (even if with different weapons),[18] the same must be said of the crafting and "establishment" of doctrines and orthodoxies within Christianity. There will be incessant struggle over the meanings and purposes of doctrinal orthodoxies—sometimes with very unfortunate consequences, at other times leading to much needed insights and clarifications.

---

understand, for example, the dynamics that led to the creedal, doctrinal definitions of Nicaea, Constantinople, and Chalcedon, as well as those of Trent and Vatican I. See Espín, *Idol and Grace.*

[18] Depending on the standing (i.e., social position of those involved in the ongoing conflict) in the given society's "historical bloc." One telling doctrinal example is that of the ordination of women in the Roman Catholic world, as clearly demonstrated in Gary Macy's *The Hidden History of Women's Ordination: Female Clergy in the Medieval West* (Oxford: Oxford University Press, 2007). See also Orlando Espín, "An Exploration into the Theology of Grace and Sin," in *From the Heart of Our People*, ed. Orlando Espín and Miguel H. Díaz (Maryknoll, NY: Orbis, 1999), 121–152.

Interculturality

Interculturality is not inculturation.[19] The latter is often supposed
to mean that a "necessary something" exists independent of a

---

[19] I have written, over the years, about interculturality. What
follows in this section is an adapted version of the reflection on
interculturality that appeared in my *Idol and Grace*, 62–73, with
some variations and the inevitable "tweaks." Anyone familiar with
the thought of philosopher Raúl Fornet-Betancourt will see here my
dependence on his work. His vast production is in Spanish, Portu-
guese, French and German. Among his books and articles, I find
indispensable Raúl Fornet-Betancourt, "Tradición, cultura, interculturalidad. Apuntes para una comprensión intercultural de la cultura,"
which was his keynote lecture (Sept. 2011) at the *XII Corredor das
ideias do Cone Sul*, Universidade do Vale dos Sinos (Unisinos), São
Leopoldo, RS, Brazil. Also very important are Fornet-Betancourt,
Transformación intercultural de la filosofía (Bilbao: Desclée de
Brouwer, 2001); Fornet-Betancourt, *Inculturalidad y religión. Para
una lectura intercultural de la crisis actual del cristianismo* (Quito: Ed.
Abya-Yala, 2007); Fornet-Betancourt, *Tareas y propuestas de la filosofía
intercultural* (Aachen: Verlag Mainz, 2009); Fornet-Betancourt, *La
interculturalidad a prueba* (Aachen: Verlag Mainz, 2006); Fornet-
Betancourt, *Interculturalidad, crítica y liberación* (Aachen: Verlag
Mainz, 2012); Fornet-Betancourt, *Interculturalidad y globalización*
(San José, Costa Rica: Departamento Ecuménico de Investigaciones,
2000); and Fornet-Betancourt, "Lo intercultural: el problema de
su definición," http://fudepa.org/Biblioteca/recursos/ficheros/
BMI20050000628/9betancour.pdf. The journal *Topologik: Rivista
Internationale di Scienze Filosofiche, Pedagogiche e Sociali* published
a special multi-language issue (no. 19, 2016, https://www.topologik.
net/Issue_19.html), with texts by twenty-three authors, on the work
of Raúl Fornet-Betancourt on intercultural philosophy and on philosophy done interculturally. That issue of *Topologik* is probably the best
introduction to this groundbreaking philosopher's thought.

culture and can be "poured" or "transmitted" into other cultures. The "necessary something" assumes, furthermore, an interpretation or understanding possible only within, and from within a dominant culture, because the "necessary something" does not interpret itself, and, therefore, does not understand or proclaim itself (or by itself) as necessary. For something in inculturation to be considered necessary implies that someone, in and from a specific cultural horizon, determined (and thus, because of a set of interests proper to the cultural horizon of the one doing the determining) that this "something" exists, and that it is definitively "necessary."

Inculturation, consequently, often includes the possibility of colonization. Inculturation thus understood has little to do with the truth that is discovered and that convinces, but rather it has to do with the acceptance of someone else's proclamation—inevitably constructed from within the proclaimer's cultural perspective—that the truth being brought to me should or must convince me because (the proclaimer believes) I need it.

The understanding of inculturation briefly suggested above, however, is not the only possible understanding, and is not descriptive of the best intentions of the best proclaimers. As Néstor Medina's incisive *Christianity, Empire and the Spirit*[20] explains in convincing detail, there are other possible understandings of inculturation (especially in contemporary Catholic perspectives) that avoid the dangers of colonization under the guise of evangelization. The appeal of these recent ecclesial understandings is to decolonize the notion of

---

[20] Néstor Medina, *Christianity, Empire and the Spirit: (Re) Configuring Faith and the Cultural* (Leiden: Brill, 2018), 220–310.

"mission," and to redefine inculturation in terms of "incarnation." Inculturation (thus redefined) more closely resembles that which has been understood as kenotic solidarity."[21]

One powerful insight in Medina's book, however, suggests that we move beyond the category of inculturation: "The Spirit's work in the cultural pushes us toward inclusion, toward the daring act of recognizing the activity of the divine in the complex interchange of cultural traditions infused by the Spirit."[22] In other words, *the pneumatological* (i.e., the action of the Spirit) *leads to the intercultural.*

Instead of "inculturation," we should perhaps say that others may "witness" to us, in an open dialogue and in lives lived, what they understand and live as truth. And we, within and from within our own cultural perspective, will contrast and perhaps assume that truth, because we have discovered it as truth within and from within our cultural horizon. And in turn, upon our discovery of truth, we will witness to the others, again in an open dialogue and in lives lived, what we have come to understand and live as truth, inviting the others to question and/or grow in what they—the others—might understand and live as truth—thereby moving the process into an ever-deepening and continuing dialogue, or potential conflict, where truth might be discovered and affirmed, reinterpreted, or rejected, for the sake of survival. This underlines

---

[21] See Medina, *Christianity, Empire and the Spirit*, 220–252, 341–342. See also Espín, *Idol and Grace*, 127–129; and Joerg Rieger, *Christ and Empire: From Paul to Postcolonial Times* (Minneapolis: Fortress, 2007), 42–44. The French term *solidarité* implies "interdependent" or "mutually dependent" to the point of being or becoming *one* (i.e., a "solid").

[22] See Medina, *Christianity, Empire and the Spirit*, 344.

that "ortholalia"[23] is not equivalent to "orthodoxy," although, as we shall see later, the former might become a necessary veil for expressing the latter.

The discovery of truth results from intercultural dialogue, and not from arguments and concepts born within a cultural horizon foreign to us and designed to convince us by pulling us away from our own cultural horizon.

The argument that truth must critique cultures cannot be made to imply or provoke colonization, or the assumed superiority of one culture over others. Such would be the implication if the understanding of truth (which is offered for acceptance by another) proceeds from a dominant culture, or from a hegemonic group within a dominant culture, which have access to the "receiving" culture precisely because of their hegemony or dominance over it, or when the critique of culture is not the historically authentic or possible fruit of the receiving culture's own possibilities.[24] That truth must critique culture is a two-way street.

Truth is a cultural and an intercultural *process*. No culture, and no cultural situation, may be considered as the definitive locus of truth, or as the best vehicle for the expression of truth. Cultures only offer us the possibilities and instruments for seeking after truth and naming it when we find it. Truth

---

[23] A neologism meaning "correct speech" used to indicate external or public acceptance of doctrine or authority. See Orlando Espín, "Ortholalia," in *Introductory Dictionary of Theology and Religious Studies*, 993.

[24] See Pierre Bourdieu, *The Field of Cultural Production* (New York: Columbia University Press, 1993), esp. 74–111 and Jacques Rancière, *The Ignorant Schoolmaster* (Stanford, CA: Stanford University Press, 1991).

will only unveil itself to us if we are willing (in intercultural dialogue) to risk "contrasting" our truth with the truth claims and/or truth expressions originating in other cultures. As anthropology and other social sciences have demonstrated, reality (and thus truth) is not "monochrome" or judged the same everywhere by everyone. Rather, reality (and thus truth) is "plurichrome."

It would be nonsense to assume, in today's world, that the truth claims of one religious or national group are "universally valid" just because this one group has (through its own cultural categories and assessment) discovered or affirmed something to be true. By "universal validity" I mean here that a truth claim, from within a specific culture, is presented to and possibly imposed on the potential recipients because the claim's birthing culture assumes its particular perspectives (that is, its questions and themes, its answers and solutions, its "facts" and evidence, its practices and approaches) to be applicable to and correct for all other cultures. The claim to universal validity has usually accompanied the history of power, hegemonic dominance, and colonization, and has been all too frequently legitimized by these.

Only in intercultural dialogue, contrasting truth claims with one another, can there begin to appear what may be said to be a universally relevant truth claim. By universal relevance, I mean that a truth claim may be offered, from within a specific culture or group, to others who may find the claim to be useful, suggestive, or even true, thereby opening for and within the recipients perspectives (questions and themes, answers and solutions, practices and approaches) that had hitherto remained closed, blurred, or unknown. It might be possible to discover common threads and denominators with universal relevance among the truth claims, but the original claim does not present itself as necessarily applicable or correct for all possible recipients and in all possible cultural contexts. The recipients must consent (from within their own cultural universes) to the relevance—partial or complete—of the claim that is offered to them. Only in the contrasting intercultural dialogue necessary for the discovery of universally relevant claims can truth be acknowledged, and only then can truth unveil itself without the trappings of empire, imposition, or idolatry.

Offering to others what we regard as true may also result in rejection or misunderstanding. But even this possibility must remind us that all claims regarding truth, whether resulting in rejection, misunderstanding, or acceptance, are still human claims, with all that every human claim implies and lacks.

It might also be important to pluck our understanding of truth from the prison of concepts. It might be important to let others, and to let truth itself, be "un-defined" for us (within our own cultural perspective), letting distinctiveness communicate with us as distinct or different and, therefore, without necessarily cleanly fitting within our categories.[25] This "in-definition" has nothing to do with relativism—on the contrary, it is the humble and realistic acceptance of our own cultural limitation and a critique of our own cultural inclination to self-idolatry.[26]

---

[25] I have borrowed this notion of the "in-definition" of truth from Fornet-Betancourt's writings and as result of personal conversations with him.

[26] The fear of relativism has been a frequent (and often successful) ideological tool in the hands of the socially and religiously dominant.

The postmodern emphasis on cultural particularity seems to have little future in our world because cultural particularities, seen from many postmodern perspectives, appear in fact to close themselves off to the world's diversity, instead of seeking to integrate diversity into the cultural particularities. Some postmodern perspectives seem to presume that diversities need not dialogue in mutually challenging, critiquing, and/or enriching ways. Confronted with the contemporary difficulty of making universally valid claims, some postmodern philosophical views on particularities have practically chosen to enclose themselves within their particular cultural worlds, giving up on the need for intercultural dialogue, while philosophically legitimizing this closing-off as the intellectually honest, academically rigorous, and best option to admit contextualization.[27] Unfortunately, some contemporary philosophers and theologians dismiss as unimportant most critical reflection on the very real power asymmetries that permit *their* thought.[28]

Fear of something, however, is not identical or coextensive with the something feared.

[27] See Aristinete B. Oliveira Neto, *Filosofía latinoamericana como política cultural. Un diálogo con Richard Rorty y Raúl Fornet-Betancourt* (Bogotá: Ed. Universidad Santo Tomás, 2014). See also Enrique Dussel, Karl-Otto Apel, and Raúl Fornet-Betancourt, *Fundamentación de la ética y la filosofía de la liberación* (Mexico City: Siglo XXI Editores, 1992).

[28] Of particular relevance is Arjun Appadurai, *The Future as Cultural Fact: Essays on the Global Condition* (London: Verso, 2013), 9–100, 269–300. See also Juan C. Scannone and Gerard Remolina, eds., *Filosofar en situación de indigencia* (Madrid: Comillas, 1984); Fernando García Cambeiro, ed., *Cultura popular y filosofía de la liberación* (Buenos Aires: Estudios Latinoamericanos, 1975); Luis

There is no one evident human universality; rather, there are multiple historical and cultural human particular universalities that can encounter one another, challenge one another, and which—through intercultural dialogue—might engage in the process of unveiling universally relevant truth. Each one of the many particular universalities acts as the platform from which a way of thought is opened and launched in the world—opening and launching each particular universality to dialogue with other particular universalities and with other truth processes. Our own particular historical, cultural universality is but the first point of reference from which to know and say what is ours, insofar as it is our concrete life and thought universe. But it is also our first point of reference in learning and perceiving the contingency of our knowing and saying. This honest discovery and acknowledgment of our contingency and transience is a *sine qua non* condition for critiquing our particular historical, cultural universality, thereby avoiding the self-idolatry of our historical, particular cultural universe. By acknowledging the contingency and transience of our particular universality (and of its experiencing, knowing, living, and saying), we open our universality to the

Martínez Andrade, "La posmodernidad: otro discurso neocolonial," *Revista del CESLA* 12 (2009): 145–152; and the excellent reflection by Enrique Dussel, *Posmodernidad y transmodernidad: Diálogos con la filosofía de Gianni Vattimo* (Mexico City: Universidad Iberoamericana, 1991). Also important are Gregor McLennan, "The Enlightenment Project Revisited," in *Modernity: An Introduction to Modern Societies*, ed. Stuart Hall et al. (Oxford: Blackwell, 1997), 644–651 and Raúl Fornet-Betancourt, ed., *Interaction and Asymmetry between Cultures in the Context of Globalization* (Frankfurt am Main: V. für Interkulturelle Kommunikation, 2002).

possibility, indeed to its need, for dialogue, for learning from other particular historical and cultural universalities, and for allowing our universality to be called to solidarity with others.

Dialogue with others and self-critique are not and cannot merely be options or possibilities (although they certainly are too). Dialogue and self-critique should be recognized as life *needs*, without which any particular cultural, historical universality simply withers into self-idolatry. Consequently, intercultural dialogue is the opposite of a dominant provincialism whereby the dominant (often white, Western) cultures decree and define their own universality as the only "universally valid" universality.[29]

Intercultural dialogue does not assume or propose any culture, any particular universality, any doctrinal construct, or any philosophical or theological current, as the best way—in any sense—for the entire world. Indeed, intercultural dialogue assumes itself to be also in need of critique, as it too acknowledges itself contingent. It holds (again, radically open to

---

[29] Colonization and dominance do not factually or ethically justify claims of universal validity frequently put forth by the Eurocentric only on behalf of their own philosophies, theologies, and methods in an attempt to ideologically legitimize their dominance. See Dipesh Chakrabarty, *Provincializing Europe: Postcolonial Thought and Historical Difference* (Princeton: Princeton University Press, 2000). I suggest the reader recall that the white beneficiaries of African slavery "found evidence" (in Bible and doctrine) that "demonstrated" their victims to be incapable of any "logical," alternative claim. The reader can reasonably suspect that today Christian discussions on race, gender, and sexual orientation are similarly infected by the logic and way of argument that infected past Christian discussions on the ethical validity of slavery, the place of Earth in the cosmos, the superiority of the "Aryan" race, and more.

correction) that the process of contrasting conversation, where all is risked in and for the sake of truth-searching dialogue, is capable of determining or clarifying what the intercultural dialogue should be and how it should be carried out.[30]

There is a need in theology (as well as in philosophy and the social sciences) to multiply and broaden the sources. This does not simply mean that we have to add to the list of sources the names and contributions of other "*objects* of study" we might have set aside in the past—although this addition might be beneficial. By multiplying and broadening the sources of theology I here mean that the voices, lives, and realities of other, as well as the previously unheard or silenced "theologizing *subjects*,"[31] must be heard and considered on an equal basis with the voices of the theologizing subjects of Europe and of the white, Eurocentric everywhere. In other words, the theologizing subjects from non-dominant communities must be positively and actively acknowledged (by themselves and by

---

[30] Consequently, an intercultural theological method can only arise from within the process and dynamics of risk-taking open, contrasting dialogues, where all are seated as equals at the same theological table "owned and served" by all, where no one is guest and all are hosts and where all are equally heard and equally engaged. An ethically credible intercultural theological method will require, consequently, that the grounding equality of all be accompanied by an honest acknowledgment and critique of dominant and/or colonized ethnocentrism(s), racism(s) and androcentrism(s) that replicate society's power asymmetries. Relevant here, although he does not explicitly speak of interculturality, is the work by Michel-Rolph Trouillot, *Silencing the Past: Power and the Production of History* (Boston: Beacon, 1995). See also Fornet-Betancourt, *Tareas y propuestas de la filosofía intercultural*, 63–94.

[31] "Subjects" and not "objects."

all others) as *being* also at the theological *con-vivencia*, and *as always having been there.* Mostly unheard and disregarded, as bearers of perspectives, alternatives, universalities, logic, and truth, *and* as theologizing subjects, the non-dominant challenge and critique what Eurocentric, "white" theologies have provincially and far from innocently assumed to be self-evident and have further and conveniently attempted to impose as "the mainstream."[32]

Intercultural thought requires that we learn to think in new ways. In other words, interculturality invites us to go beyond attempts at "enriching" our own perspectives by somehow incorporating the contributions of others, because this enrichment approach would ultimately leave our

---

[32] Few theologians, in the US or elsewhere, have been as convincing and thorough in their critique and unmasking of the "erasing, dismissing, and silencing" power dynamics, in US theology, as Carmen Nanko-Fernández. See her *Theologizing en Espanglish: Context, Community and Ministry* (Maryknoll, NY: Orbis, 2010). See also Nanko-Fernández, "Alternately Documented Theologies: Mapping Border, Exile and Diaspora," in *Religion and Politics in America's Borderlands*, ed. Sarah Azaransky (Lanham, MD: Lexington, 2013), 33–55; Nanko-Fernández, "We Are Not Your Diversity, We Are the Church! Ecclesiological Reflections from the Marginalized Many," *Perspectivas* (Fall 2006): 81–107; Nanko-Fernández, "¡Cuidado! The Church Who Cares and Pastoral Hostility," *New Theology Review* (Feb. 2006): 24–33; Nanko-Fernández, "Signs of the Times: Not Just a Game," *New Theology Review* 24:3 (2011): 73–75; and Nanko-Fernández, "Creation in Divine Diversity: Imaging Community, Respecting Difference," *New Theology Review* 24:2 (May 2011): 27–38. At the gathering for the 25th anniversary (2016) of the National Catholic Council of Hispanic Ministry, Nanko-Fernández's address was an extraordinarily insightful proposal of a "Pneumatology of ¡Basta Ya!"

assumptions and methods untouched and uncritiqued, since it would be through them that we enrich what already is. What is new in the way of intercultural thinking is found in risking our assumptions, certainties, and methods by dialogically contrasting them with the assumptions, certainties, and methods of others, and through this contrasting dialogue being willing to give up some or many of our assumptions and methods and to acquire new ones encountered in and through the intercultural contrasting dialogue.[33] We are thus called to learn to see ourselves, our cultural particular universalities, our histories, and our lives, as well as our theological assumptions and methods, in the new light offered to us by those who are culturally different from us. The new way of intercultural thinking is thus polyphonic, as it would ultimately lead us to see our theology—as well as our cultures, societies, and histories—as bound and related to and with others, thereby negating the temptation to self-enclosing idolatry, dissimulated hegemonic dominance, and/or culturally invented relativism.

Once again we must recall that theology—indeed, all of Christianity—occurs only in this world as this world exists. Today a de-contextualized dialogue (or one that does not begin by acknowledging and facing the dimensions impinging on its credibility as ethically honest search for

---

[33] I find pertinent the work biblical scholar Carleen Mandolfo has done on "dialogic criticism" and the work of Mikhail Bakhtin. For example, see Carleen Mandolfo, "Finding Their Voices: Sanctioned Subversion in Psalms of Lament," *Horizons in Biblical Theology* 24, no. 2 (May 2002): 27–52. This article includes notes and references to works by Bakhtin, and by others on Bakhtin's work, specifically focusing on his call for dialogic criticism.

truth) would be an ideological exercise only benefiting those favored by hegemony.

The sacralization of any culture (given every culture's internal history of conflict) would itself contradict intercultural dialogue and instead suggest idolatry disguised as scholarship or orthodoxy. This is one reason why intercultural thought has much to offer theology, and to the global study and hermeneutic of doctrines. And to pneumatology in a new key.

Time and Transience

We are all in time. Every living being on Earth and elsewhere, and every insect, every rock, every planet, every star, every constellation: all are in time. And yes, it is still necessary to assert the obvious: that because of time, nothing is permanent or unchangeable. Everything and everyone is transient. There is no escape.[34] *Dios perdona, pero el tiempo a ninguno.* Time, however, is never lived, experienced or acknowledged except in *place*— also inescapably limited and passing. It is in and from within our human places (*topoi*) that we experience, relate, and understand.

Time and place, it seems, are the two sides of reality whose embodied interactions conceive (in the sense of making

---

[34] We notice and experience time as passing, as transience. This awareness results from the several biorhythms of/in our bodies, and in the bodies of all living beings, and from the observable "movements" of celestial bodies. Time seems to be the human perception of *our* undeniable and inescapable transience from birth to death. We have learned to measure time, but our measurements are not time and cannot themselves escape transience. The Spanish phrase cited in the text above is from the lyrics of a song ("*Abrázame*") by the late Mexican composer and singer Juan Gabriel.

possible in time and place, not of mere conceptualizing) cultures, understandings, history, power relations, religions, and much more.

Consequently, no human claim can pretend permanence, absoluteness, or irreformability. Whatever we might regard as "objective" or "definitive" cannot, and does not, cancel its transience. Time and transience are the ultimate antidotes to human hubris and inclination to self-idolatry, and the ultimate argument against the socially dominant pretension that unjust, inhumane socio-economic and political structures, built on societies' non-innocent notions of gender, race, class, age, ethnicity, etc., are somehow permanent, "divinely sanctioned," or "natural." Injustice and unjust structures[35] are choices and/or the result of choices made by those with the power to make and normalize them as "obvious" or "natural."

How do we craft our cultures in time and transience? By memory and interpretation—in other words, by history. Which means that human meaningfulness—i.e., culture—is non-innocent because it rests on memory and interpretive choices made by those with the power to determine what is history.[36]

---

[35] There are unjust structures that normalize, perpetuate, and provoke poverty, lack of access to education and healthcare, lack of available healthy food and of adequate housing. There are unjust structures that create and militarize borders between nations, and then create zones of "legal" violence and abuse in the name of national security. There are also unjust structures that impose rules for the benefit of interests represented by the legislating classes. And a long list of etceteras. What is legal or illegal is not coextensive with what is moral or immoral, and it has never been.

[36] Insights from Ignacio Ellacuría are present here, especially

History is not coextensive with time or transience. History is not a given but a crafted interpretation of ourselves (of *our* past, to help us understand *our* present, and to suggest how to build *our* future in order to achieve *our* interests—all requiring an ethically non-innocent understanding of "we" and "our," i.e., of *our* identity). Of the trillions of events that have occurred and continue to occur in every moment of time, we have chosen to remember a tiny fraction, because we have decided that these few (events, "facts," and beings) are meaningful for us to understand who *we* are, how *we* should be and act, and how and why *we* relate to others, and to make our resulting identities appear "evidently stable" (to us). However, because memory (individual, social, cultural, and ecclesial) is selective, it is an ethical or unethical construct, or both. Memory is arguably important, but never absolute, immutable, or total. Consequently, we have

---

from his *Filosofía de la realidad histórica* (San Salvador: UCA Editores, 1990), chap. 2, 3, 4, and 5 (esp. chap. 4, sec. 3, and all of chap. 5); insights are present also from Ellacuría, *Escritos filosóficos* (San Salvador: UCA Editores, 1996–2001), esp. vols. 2 and 3; and from Ellacuría, *Escritos teológicos* (San Salvador: UCA Editores, 2000–02), esp. vol. 2, chap. 5, sect. 5.2 and 5.3. Nevertheless, my perspectives on history are not directly from Ellacuría, even though I acknowledge the influence of his thought on mine. I consider myself far from some of his assertions regarding history and from many of his philosophically grounding reflections. I am not a disciple of Xavier Zubiri's philosophy, as Ellacuría was. The best introduction to and summary of Ellacuría's philosophical thought in any language, by his most prominent disciple, intellectual heir, and successor, is Héctor Samour, *Voluntad de liberación: La filosofía de Ignacio Ellacuría* (Granada: Editorial Comares, 2003). Samour's own (broader) philosophical work is important, and very much necessary when attempting to interpret Ellacuría's and his context.

to acknowledge that "history" represents the choices of those with the hegemonic power to make history.

In other words, *the vast majority of events and human beings—just as real as the few that are remembered—are ignored, have been forgotten, and/or have had their importance dismissed* from our memory because it was decided that it be so—for our interests, if we conveniently or naïvely assume our interests and understanding of human meaningfulness to be coextensive with the interests and understanding of human meaningfulness of the hegemonically dominant. But if "we" were coextensive with the immense majority of humanity (in our societies and/or in others), then we must acknowledge that the events and beings we might or do regard as important have been ignored, forgotten, or marginalized in the memory of the dominant few, and fed to us by the cultural means hegemony employs in order to convince the real, vast majority of the "necessity" and "obviousness" of the arguments and interpretations from the real, dominant minority.[37]

Absence from, or unimportance in, human memory is the result of ongoing selection by the ones who shape(d) that particular memory.[38] It is not absence from what some think is "objective history" because "objective history" is only the limited result of a culturally constructed selection by those who had the socio-cultural, hegemonic power to select what is or is not important. "Objective history" is selective and non-innocent memory, organized and interpreted by the

---

[37] See Gruppi, *O conceito de hegemonia em Gramsci.*

[38] Michel de Certeau's thought, manifestly, stands behind much of my reflection on "history," especially Michel de Certeau, *L'Absent de l'histoire* (Paris: Mame, 1973) and de Certeau, *L'Écriture de l'histoire* (Paris: Gallimard, 1975).

hegemonically dominant, in order to convince (both themselves and the non-dominant) that their hegemonic selection from among the trillions of events and beings is *the* reality, *the* important humans, and *the* events to remember, and *the* meaningfulness of *the* world, now made to be coextensive with theirs.[39] The immense majority of humankind is consequently absent from "history."

Christianity and its doctrines, rituals, ethical expectations, biblical interpretations, ecclesial polities, and histories, occur in time, are all inescapably transient, and are selected, crafted, believed in, performed, and remembered within the context of selective, non-innocent memory and history that I have summarized above. There is no escape from this conclusion. Christian doctrines, rituals, symbols, ecclesial polities, biblical interpretations, and histories, therefore, also display dominant selections by those with power to establish doctrines, symbols, etc., as true and good, and even as "revealed."

I am not suggesting or saying that this dynamic within Christianity is of necessity intrinsically evil, unworthy, or polluted. What I am very clearly saying, however, is that Christians are human and, therefore, inescapably bound by time, transience, and the non-innocent processes that produce "history"—including "church history."

Some Christians might be shocked or embarrassed to admit that they too are evidently as limited and perspectival (and as non-innocent) as the rest of the human race, but that is irrelevant to my argument. What is relevant is that all of our

---

[39] See Beatriz Sarlo, *Tiempo pasado: Cultura de la memoria y giro subjetivo* (Buenos Aires: Siglo XXI, 1996); Sarlo, *Tiempo presente* (Buenos Aires: Siglo XXI, 2001) and Sarlo, *Scenes from Postmodern Life* (Minneapolis: University of Minnesota Press, 2001).

doctrines, rituals, biblical interpretations, symbols, ecclesial polities, and histories came to be accepted as Christian because someone had the power to establish them as such. Hegemony and dominance, and their concomitant marginalization of the immense majority of Christians and their forced absence from "church history," are part of Christian experience.[40] Power is not intrinsically evil or destructive, but it is (again inescapably) ethically non-innocent and always guided by interests.

What we refer to as orthodoxy, and orthodox doctrines, were elaborated—frequently as part of the resolution for a conflictive period within the Church—and established as "orthodox" by those who had the power within or over the Church. But for whose interests?

To naïvely claim that these doctrinal decisions or teachings were always intended for the "good" of the Church or in fidelity to the "faith" of the Church is to adulterate the facts and the faith—unless one cares to walk onto the theological, doctrinal precipice of identifying "the Church" with "the ordained."

---

[40] It is undeniable that the majority of Christians, over the past twenty centuries, have been illiterate. Yet they, who are and have been the Church, have too often been marginalized ("made to be absent") from the theological and doctrinal conversations within the institutional Church. The importance of the illiteracy of the People cannot be dismissed when theologians and the ordained go around discussing Tradition, beliefs, or faith while ignoring or downplaying the faith, beliefs, and ways of "traditioning" employed by the illiterate and the poor, who have been the demonstrable vast *majority* of the (*real*) Church. What theologians and the ordained have often regarded as "Tradition" has too conveniently reflected the cultures, race, gender, and interests of the socially and culturally dominant. See Espín, *Idol and Grace*, 40–44 and Espín, *Grace and Humanness*, 15–50. See again Gruppi, *O Conceito de hegemonia em Gramsci*.

Two very important examples, from the many possible. First: During several centuries, common doctrinal teaching among the ordained legitimized the enslavement of African and African-descendant persons, who were regarded (appealing to biblical texts and to Greek philosophy) as intrinsically inclined to servitude by nature—and hence, by God.[41] Second: For centuries, the military conquest of lands and subsequent genocides of the Native peoples of the Americas were held as legitimate because of the "missionary" expansion offered to the Church and the "salvation" brought to the Native peoples.[42]

---

[41] See Gilberto Freyre, *Casa-grande e senzala*, 48th ed. (Recife: Global Editora, 2003); Hugh Thomas, *The Slave Trade: The Story of the Atlantic Slave Trade* (New York: Touchstone, 1997); and Francisco J. de Jaca, *Resolución sobre la libertad de los negros y sus originarios, en estado de paganos y después ya cristianos* (Madrid: Consejo Superior de Investigaciones Científicas / Instituto Francisco de Vitoria, 2002; original pub. 1682).

[42] See Juan Ginés de Sepúlveda, *Demócrates Segundo, o, De las justas causas de las guerras contra los indios* (Madrid: Consejo Superior de Investigaciones Científicas-Instituto Francisco de Vitoria, 1984; original pub. 1550) and Enrique Dussel, *1492. El encubrimiento del otro* (Madrid: Nueva Utopía, 1993). This non-innocent argument, profoundly Eurocentric and colonizing, was unfortunately (and again) employed by Benedict XVI in his inaugural Address (sec. 1) at the opening session of the Latin American bishops' Fifth General Conference, in Aparecida, Brazil, in 2007. See also the important article by Néstor Medina, "The Doctrine of Discovery, LatinaXo Theoethics, and Human Rights," *Journal of Hispanic/Latinoax Theology* 21, no. 2 (2019): 157–173. The argument that justifies the use of violence and depredation against entire peoples in order to "open them" to the Gospel is in itself a blatant adulteration of the Gospel.

In these two cases,[43] *whose* faith and *whose* interests were identified as "*the* faith" of the Church, as "*the* good" of the Church, and even as "*the* Church"?

These two examples are relevant here, because slavery, conquest, colonization, and Eurocentric missionaries and missionary efforts in the midst of the horrific realities of slavery, conquest, and colonization have very much affected and shaped the cultures, societies, and histories from which today's Latinoax come—as well as shaped and impacted their understandings and expressions of Catholicism.

A third important example: The European-American world seems to have erased from its shared memory—from "history" as it has crafted it to coincide with its interests—that when Florida, the US Southwest, and Puerto Rico entered US "history" (after undeniable US military conquests) the peoples already in these lands were never consulted and their will was dismissed as insignificant in the process of conquest and annexation. The dominant in the US have erased from "history" the fact that nearly half of the country's territory was acquired by military force and violence and against the will of the peoples living there. The US dominant have also conveniently forgotten that all of the country's land was violently taken earlier from Native peoples, again against their will. This land was then made to produce wealth for the new occupiers by the forced labor of millions of enslaved Africans. When European American "history" waxes

---

[43] There were a few exceptions among bishops and among ordained and lay missionaries (e.g., Montesinos, Las Casas, Quiroga, Jaca, Moiráns, Varela) but the exceptions only demonstrate what was the rule of the vast majority.

eloquent about this being the land of freedom, equality, and justice, it is reasonable and ethically necessary to ask: Whose freedom, equality, and justice? Whose interests are served by such selective non-innocent forgetting and remembering?

These examples of how "history" is non-innocent are important because most of today's Latinoax descend from the peoples who preceded and were conquered by the US military annexation of Florida, of the Southwest, and of Puerto Rico. To make this example as clear as possible, let us also remember that today's Latinoax are themselves the fruit of even earlier military occupations, of conquests of Native peoples, of the enslavement of Africans, and of Iberian landless peasants—also erased from memory—who often were among the "disposables" of even earlier conquests. Whose interests are served by the continued loud silences and ineffective and meaningless gestures of most bishops and theologians in the current US immigration and xenophobic crises affecting millions of their fellow Catholics and in the dangerous perpetuation of racism and racist violence in US society?[44]

What does "orthodoxy" actually measure, affirm, or assure, when the real lives and commitments of the "orthodox" seem unaffected by their claimed adherence to the Gospel? And when their "orthodox" understanding of Christianity seems untouched by *the real lives of the real Church*? How can these "orthodox" be truly Christian when

---

[44] We could also add the repeated violent, cruel acts against LGBTQ persons, fueled by religiously legitimized, homophobic attackers, that seem less ethically troublesome to many Christians than the marriage between two persons of the same gender who truly love each other. Which of God's children are "disposable" in some Christian orthodoxies?

they so blatantly dismiss as unimportant to their faith the real lives of most of humanity?

What *is* orthodox is what expresses the faith of the Church. Orthodox doctrine expresses the faith of the Church. It acts as the historical (but not timeless or de-contextualized) cultural standard of cultural expressions. But orthodoxy is not the faith of the Church. *The faith of the Church may be expressed through it, but it is not coextensive with it.* In fact, the meaning and content of "the faith of the Church" rests entirely on *who is* the Church. Faith is a life option and a life lived as a consequence of that option, and not mere assent to doctrines.

In other words, if "the Church is the People,"[45] then it follows logically that the faith of the People *is* "the faith of the Church." Which logically further leads us to affirm that "orthodox" doctrinal expressions of the faith cannot violate, dismiss, or adulterate "the faith of the People."

I am not suggesting that doctrine pollutes faith. Instead, I am focusing on the following questions: How do we deal with, and how do we theologically explain, situations in which supposedly orthodox doctrines have been used as instruments to marginalize or persecute people or force them into morally questionable (social, political, cultural) compliance? How do

---

[45] Vatican II, *Dogmatic Constitution on the Church: Lumen Gentium*, 9–13 (ch. 2). Chapter 2 of *Lumen Gentium*, titled "The People of God," stresses the equality and unity of all the Church's members. See also Daniel J. Finucane, *Sensus Fidelium: The Use of a Concept in the Post-Vatican II Era* (San Francisco: International Scholars, 1996). This work by Finucane is a theological *tour de force* on the development and use of the concept of *sensus fidelium* throughout the past twenty centuries and its indispensable function in the understanding and life of the *ekklesia*.

we deal with, and how do we theologically explain, situations in which the People have created their own (alternative) expressions of and for their faith, and yet these are dismissed because the culturally and/or ecclesiastically dominant claim that they do not find the People's expressions "clear" or "precise" enough (i.e., for the literate, elite standards of the hegemonic)? How can we theologically ignore the fact that most Christians over the last twenty centuries have been illiterate and poor?[46] How

---

[46] It seems that literacy was not widespread in Europe prior to the late 1700s and in most of the rest of the world, not even into the late 1800s. Obviously, there have been literate persons in Europe since antiquity, but that is not the point here. We are referring, instead, to the majority of ancient and medieval Europeans and to the urban and rural poor after the Reformations, and to the majority of the population during and after the Industrial Revolution. Furthermore, and much more important to the present volume, with and after the sixteenth century it is clear that Catholicism fast became a global church, with most members outside Europe, while in most of the non-European Catholic world, literacy was not (and is often still not) as common and frequent as one might think or hope. (Exceptions, of course, do exist). Consider also that across much of the world, girls and women are still often denied an education today and that racial/ethnic minorities frequently suffer the same lack of access to education. According to UNESCO, as late as the mid-1800s only ten percent of the world's adult population could read or write. For this data, and for a synthesis of the history and present reality of literacy and illiteracy across the world, see UNESCO, *Education for All: 2006 Global Monitoring Report*, chap. 8, esp. 190–213. According to the 2015 report, forty percent of the entire world is still illiterate. All UNESCO *Education Global Monitoring Reports* are online at en.unesco.org. See also Alan Bowman and Greg Woolf, eds., *Literacy and Power in the Ancient World* (Cambridge: Cambridge University Press, 1994). It is clear that progress is being made today toward an

can the People express *their* faith through *their* own means, in contexts of slavery, conquest, colonization, injustice, marginalization, and depredation? Is orthodoxy measurable by the ideological colonization of the conquered?

Lived Experience, Expressions, and Doctrine

Faith precedes doctrine, and it is not exhausted by it or coextensive with it.[47] Faith precedes doctrine in experience, in time,

---

entirely literate world, but this was not the case during nearly two thousand years of Christian history, during which the vast majority of Christians (hence, of the Church) were illiterate. This questions many of the means the dominant have assumed as necessary for the "traditioning" of Christianity, as well as exposes dynamics and locations of many arguments debated by all sides of the sixteenth-century reformations and counter-reformations.

[47] I continue to find insightful and important Alistair E. McGrath's *The Genesis of Doctrine: A Study in the Foundations of Doctrinal Criticism* (Grand Rapids: Eerdmans, 1997). Equally insightful and pertinent have been the three volumes of Justo L. González, *A History of Christian Thought* (Nashville: Abingdon, 1987) as well as Anthony C. Thiselton, *The Hermeneutics of Doctrine* (Grand Rapids, MI: Eerdmans, 2007). Two works by the late sociologist and philosopher of religion Otto Maduro not only are pertinent to a discussion on doctrine and culture, but help to provide fundamental building blocks for a non-dominant, critical hermeneutic of doctrine: Otto Maduro, *Mapas para la fiesta: Reflexiones latinoamericanas sobre la crisis y el conocimiento* (Buenos Aires: Nueva Tierra, 1993) and Maduro, *Religión y conflicto social en América Latina* (Mexico City: Centro de Estudios Ecuménicos, 1980). Maduro addresses realities, processes, and contexts necessary for the marginalized's construction of knowledge and of their truth claims, which Alistair McGrath, Anthony Thiselton, and George Lindbeck seem to

and in Christian history. This precedence leads us to consider several issues regarding human expressions[48] that are means to refer to lived experiences that then lead to doctrines regarding God and God's revelation.

In the usual Catholic use of the term, "faith" includes sincere acceptance of, and submission and life's response to revelation. But it is crucially important to underline that Catholicism understands "revelation" to *be* Jesus the Christ.[49] Catholicism claims that *Jesus* is God's definitive *self*-revelation to and in the world.[50] Consequently, "faith" is *first and foremost*

---

ignore or disregard—most likely because they are deemed to be "mere" expressions or claims of the "uneducated." I have also found important and pertinent Rubén Rosario Rodríguez, *Dogmatics after Babel: Beyond Theologies of Word and Culture* (Louisville: Westminster John Knox, 2018).

[48] Orality and literacy are not the only human means for "saying" something. I am here referring to those means neither oral nor written but which are capable of conveying, expressing, and making understandable a message or the meaning of an experience, e.g. visual arts, music, dance.

[49] See Vatican II, *Dei Verbum*, 2, 4.

[50] Karl Rahner has reflected on the meaning and implications of revelation as God's *self*-revelation, which is also God's *self*-donation. Which also implies that creation itself is revelatory of God. In Rahner's work, pneumatology and grace are mutually imbricating, as undeniably as in his insight that the human is who God is when God donates Godself outside of the trinitarian divine. Therefore, the notion of *kenosis* is fundamental in Rahner's understanding of revelation. See Karl Rahner, *Content of Faith: The Best of Karl Rahner's Theological Writings* (New York: Crossroad, 1993), esp. 47; Rahner, "Concepción teológica del hombre," in Karl Rahner et al., *Sacramentum Mundi* (Barcelona: Herder, 1976), 3:493–504; and Rahner, *Foundations of Christian Faith* (New York: Crossroad, 1982), 26–42,

entrusting, risking with, and committing one's entire life to the God revealed in Jesus, and to that God's will. "Faith," therefore, is suspect when it is dismissive or devoid of real and demonstrably committed compassionate solidarity. A "faith" that promises to "save" but leaves the suffering of the world untouched and dismissed is not faith. It is not Christian.

I have elsewhere written[51] that to affirm that God has revealed Godself in Jesus (as Christianity claims) is to claim the definitive *kairos*. And it is also to affirm that revelation is, first and foremost, God's *self*-donation: God's *kenosis*. In other words, revelation is God's self-revelation in God's scandalous self-donation. Hence, the revelatory *kairos* is also the scandalous *kenosis*.[52] Why scandalous? Because the Christian

---

75–81, and esp. 117–133. Insightful and fruitful commentary on Rahner's thought on grace, revelation, and humanness is Miguel H. Díaz, *On Being Human: Hispanic and Rahnerian Perspectives* (Maryknoll, NY: Orbis, 2001).

[51] See Espín, *Idol and Grace*, 84–93.

[52] See, for example, Phil. 2:7 and 2 Cor. 6:2. The reader should be aware that my understanding and use of the Greek term *kairos* has been influenced by both Paul's use of the term in his New Testament texts and Agamben's use(s) of the term—in turn influenced by the work of Walter Benjamin. See Giorgio Agamben, *"What Is an Apparatus?" and Other Essays* (Stanford: Stanford University Press, 2009); Agamben, *The Coming Community* (Minneapolis: University of Minnesota Press, 1993); and especially Agamben, *The Time That Remains: A Commentary on the Letter to the Romans* (Stanford: Stanford University Press, 2005). Benjamin's notion of "messianic time" is behind much of Agamben's reflections on this point, on *kairos*, and on his reinterpretation of both (messianic time and *kairos*) through each other. Therefore, see also Walter Benjamin, "Theses on the Philosophy of History," in Walter Benjamin, *Illuminations* (New York: Shocken, 1968), 253–264.

claim that God's revelation *is* Jesus of Nazareth cannot dismiss, downplay or overlook that the Jesus of Christians was a landless peasant, with all (e.g., marginalization, poverty, social vulnerability, invisibility) that this "social location" would have implied and assumed in Roman-occupied Palestine.[53]

Revelation is neither theory nor doctrine.[54] Therefore,

---

[53] See William R. Herzog, *Prophet and Teacher: An Introduction to the Historical Jesus* (Louisville: Westminster/John Knox, 2005); Herzog, *Parables as Subversive Speech: Jesus as Pedagogue of the Oppressed* (Louisville: Westminster/John Knox, 1994); and Herzog, *Jesus, Justice, and the Reign of God* (Louisville: Westminster/John Knox, 2000); John Dominic Crossan, *The Historical Jesus: The Life of a Mediterranean Jewish Peasant* (San Francisco: HarperCollins, 1992); Crossan, *Jesus: A Revolutionary Biography* (San Francisco: HarperCollins, 1994); Richard Horsley, *Jesus and Empire: The Kingdom of God and the New World Order* (Minneapolis: Fortress, 2002); Horsley, *Galilee: History, Politics, People* (Valley Forge: Trinity Press International, 1995); and Horsley, *Archaeology, History and Society in Galilee: The Social Context of Jesus and the Rabbis* (Valley Forge: Trinity Press International, 1996). See also Wolfgang Stegemann, Bruce Malina, and Gerd Theissen, eds., *The Social Setting of Jesus and the Gospels* (Minneapolis: Fortress, 2002); Bruce Malina, *The Social World of Jesus and the Gospels* (New York: Routledge, 1996); and emphatically, Manuel Fraijó, *Jesús y los marginados* (Madrid: Cristiandad, 1985); Carlos Bravo, *Galilea, año 30. Historia de un conflicto* (Mexico City: Centro de Reflexión Teológica, 1989); and Hugo Echegaray, *La práctica de Jesús* (Lima: Centro de Estudios y Publicaciones, 1980).

[54] The First Vatican Council (1869–70), responding to issues critical to the nineteenth century, considered that revelation was a series of "supernatural truths" that God revealed to humans, requiring the "submission of the intellect" (in Vatican I's understanding of faith) to these revealed truths. But the idea of revelation as propositional is culturally impossible and religiously untenable. The Second Vatican Council (1962–65), on the other hand, went clearly well

faith is our response to Jesus as revelation, but not a response focused on or limited to assent to doctrines about Jesus or that are claimed to have come from Jesus. Faith is our self-committing and self-implicating response to the defiant alternative that earliest Christianity held to have been the core message announced by Jesus: i.e., that God *is* transforming *this* world according to God's compassionate will, thereby constructing a drastically different world *here*.

To respond in faith to this defiant, subversive message, defiantly lived by this landless Jewish Galilean peasant, requires a commitment to live one's life accordingly—i.e., in the manner of Jesus, in order to actively witness to and help make real God's world-transforming alternative. This faith rests on the reasonable hope that a world drastically built on compassionate solidarity and justice is a world according to the will of God. Faith, as response, is the wager of our lives for and with God's defiance of the *status quo*.

The above discussion on faith, of course, brings up the question of salvation. To be coherent, if one understands Jesus as the self-revelation and self-donation of God, and if one recognizes that his core message was about God's transformation of this world into a world without oppression, then whatever we understand as "salvation" cannot be focused exclusively on, or made coextensive with, an otherworldly reality after death. If whatever we mean by salvation does not first and foremost, and explicitly, include the reality of *this* world

---

beyond Vatican I by emphasizing the historical character of revelation, its definitive fullness *being* Jesus the Christ, and by reaffirming the biblical understanding of "faith" as entrusting one's life to God in response to Jesus and his core message.

without injustice and without oppression, then that salvation is as suspect as a "faith" without compassionate solidarity.

To interpret salvation exclusively by the otherworldly is to eviscerate the core message of Jesus of Nazareth and to miss the meaning of the biblical expressions "Day of the Lord" and "Reign of God." The *eschata* (the "last things") are last because present reality carries within it the seeds of its definitive tomorrow as those seeds' actual fruition. The "last things" are at the end of *this* history and *this* world because they stand at the moment of fulfillment of the already-begun *final* history and *final* world, radically fulfilled as a "new creation." Christians believe and hope that the fulfillment of our best in time will be (and already has begun to be) made possible by God, but by the God who does not deny the Incarnation as trade-off for an otherworldly salvation.

No matter how consoling the hope of eternity might be for many (i.e., hope of "saving their souls"), the core message of Jesus as witnessed by the New Testament was about God's will for this world, and the transformation of this world according to the divine will, and our required behavior in this world on behalf of the world's victims. Salvation is from this world as currently structured according to human greed, abuse, and oppression. But salvation from this world, from its sin, cannot be reduced to a consoling escape into eschatological individualism that leaves this world in its sinful structures of oppression, as if these and their victims were ultimately irrelevant to God and Gospel, and irrelevant to the everyday lives of Christians. Salvation, on the contrary, is *for this world radically transformed* by God's empowerment.[55]

---

[55] Conversations with professors Russell Fuller and Peter Mena,

Faith precedes doctrine, rendering doctrine ancillary to faith's hoped-for outcome: salvation as this world radically transformed according to God's compassionate will for justice, inclusion, and equality, without limits, conditions, or exceptions. A life lived on behalf of the "new world" God wills is immensely more important than the doctrinal explanations (even the "normative" ones) we craft.

But doctrines we have. Sometimes they have been instruments of abuse, but other times they have been helpful, clarifying means in conversations and debates among Christians. Pneumatological doctrines have been no exception.

In pneumatology too, faith precedes doctrine and theology. Which raises the question of how we can speak of the Holy Spirit without first assuming the doctrine that there *is* a Holy Spirit. Can we arrive at pneumatological faith prior to pneumatological doctrinal, theological discourse?[56] What

---

my colleagues at the University of San Diego, have importantly contributed to my thought and discussion of "salvation."

[56] This section and other parts of this chapter have been enriched by the work of Timothy J. Gorringe, especially his *Furthering Humanity: A Theology of Culture* (Burlington, VT: Ashgate, 2004); and more importantly by conversations with the work of Néstor Medina, in particular his *Christianity, Empire and the Spirit*; and Néstor Medina, "Discerning the Spirit in Culture: Toward Pentecostal Interculturality," *Canadian Journal of Pentecostal-Charismatic Christianity* 2 (2010); Medina, "Unlikely Siblings? Pentecostal Insights from the Catholic Teachings on Mary," in *Third Receptive Ecumenism Conference Proceedings*, ed. Paul Murray and Paul Lakeland (Oxford: Oxford University Press, forthcoming); Néstor Medina, "Theological Musings toward a Latina/o/x Pneumatology" in *The Wiley-Blackwell Companion to Latinoax Theology*, 2nd ed. (Hoboken, NJ: Wiley, 2023), 173–190; and Medina, "The Pneumatological Dimension of

experiences may Christians have had (or believed others had) that led them to express the seeds of what in time became pneumatology?

What lived experiences might Christians point to as birthing locations for their belief and affirmations that there is a Holy Spirit? To answer briefly: *experiences of empowerment and effective solidarity.*

The Hebrew Bible speaks of *ruach*, and more specifically of the *ruach* of and from God. But *ruach*, spirit, is breath, wind, the winds of change, the breath of life, and even the internal disposition or inclination of a person. *Ruach* (in the Hebrew Scriptures) typically acts as instrument or agent of God, in nature as well as in human hearts, to empower, to move, and to make happen.[57] And although frequently associated with christology (especially in and since the Johannine writings), the Hebrew term *shekinah* is also relevant to pneumatology because the *ruach* of God does not leave the people orphaned—God dwells among them and is actively present to them.[58]

Orlando Espín's Theological Work and Its Implications for Engagement with Pentecostal Communities," *Journal of Hispanic/Latino Theology* (2010). Relevant for a pneumatology is the careful consideration of Carleen Mandolfo and Nancy C. Lee, eds., *Lamentations in Ancient and Contemporary Cultural Contexts* (Atlanta: Society of Biblical Literature, 2008).

[57] The Hebrew Scriptures and the New Testament sometimes refer to and personify "wisdom," thereby making possible its later use in Christian pneumatological reflections as well as in christological ones. Russian Orthodox theologians (e.g., Bulgakov and Solovyov) have revived "wisdom's" pneumatological connections. See also Elisabeth Schüssler Fiorenza, *Jesus: Miriam's Child, Sophia's Prophet. Critical Issues in Feminist Christology* (New York: Continuum, 1994).

[58] *Shekinah* does not appear in the Hebrew Bible, but it does

Similar to *ruach* in its meanings is the New Testament term *pneuma*. The Johannine corpus also uses *parakletos*, a term meaning one who helps, comforts, empowers, or pleads for. *Parakletos* is one who "stands with," in active solidarity.[59]

None of these nouns originally referred exclusively to God,[60] but since early Christianity these three terms have been used to describe experiences of God and the God encountered in these experiences.

The earliest Christians came mostly from peasant, urban poor, and even slavery contexts. Most Christians throughout the following twenty centuries have been poor, illiterate, and generally marginal to those who literally "made history." In other words, most Christians in the world have been, and demonstrably still are, vulnerable and disposable to the

---

appear in rabbinic literature to speak of God's "dwelling" among the people too (as "presence," which the New Testament will later refer to as *doxa*, "glory"). See Ephraim E. Urbach, *The Sages: Their Concepts and Beliefs* (Jerusalem: Hebrew University/Magnes Press, 1975), 37–65.

59 On uses of *ruach*, See Gen.1:2; Exod. 36:1ff.; Judg. 14:6; Isa. 11:2; Isa. 42:1; Isa. 61:1ff.; Ezek. 36:26ff; Ps. 51:11; Joel 2:28–32; Sir. 39:6; Wisd. 7;7 and 9:17; etc. On uses of *pneuma*, See Mark. 1:10; Mark 1:12; Mark 13:11; Matt. 1:18,20; Matt. 10:20; Matt. 12:18; Luke. 1:35; Luke 12:12; Acts 2:1–33; Acts 8: 15–17; Acts 11:12; Acts 15:28; Acts 16:6ff.; Acts 19:6; Phil. 1:19; Rom. 8:9–11,26; Rom. 12; Gal. 4:6; Gal. 5; 1 Cor. 2; 1 Cor. 3:16; 1 Cor. 6:17; 1 Cor. 7:40; 1 Cor. 12; 1 Cor. 14; 1 Cor. 15:42–44. On uses of *parakletos*, See John 14:16–17; throughout John 14–16; and 1 John 2:1; etc.

60 *Ruach* is a feminine term, as is *shekinah*; *pneuma* is neuter, and *parakletos* is masculine. The grammatical gender of terms is relevant when discussing whom is "said" through them, because the grammatically masculine gender, in pneumatology, is clearly neither necessary nor exclusive nor the more frequent in Hebrew or Greek.

dominant who craft their memories into "history" and who continue to benefit from centuries of power asymmetries.[61]

It is not surprising, therefore, that among most Christians (including the earliest generations), God was experienced as "empowering." The seemingly impossible—i.e., the transformation of *this* world into one of justice and solidarity—has become *possible* and unavoidable, because God empowers us to make it possible. God promises that the new world will be a reality. We—who had thought ourselves incapable of radically transforming the realities of hegemony and power asymmetries—can now do, by God's will and empowerment, the seemingly impossible and create a radically new world *here*.

The indispensable empowering experience of God has very frequently been expressed through, and implied in, the several meanings of *ruach*, *pneuma*, and *parakletos*. The faith of Christians was and is in a compassionately[62] solidarious, life-giving, comforting, and empowering God, *self*-revealed in a Galilean Jewish peasant and in his defiant life and death, and whose will is the transformation of the world into one where "God

---

[61] Also, during most of the last twenty centuries, many of the beneficiaries of history and its power asymmetries have called themselves Christian as well. Their numbers in any generation, however, have been minuscule when compared to the millions of vulnerable Christians and non-Christians marginalized and regarded as disposable. I again remind the reader that today the majority of Christians are not in Europe or North America. This too is the specific case of Catholic Christianity: the majority of Catholics are not in Europe and in European-descendant North America. In US Catholicism, the majority has ceased to be white European-descendants.

[62] The Latin *compassio*, etymologically, means "enduring with."

reigns." In this defiant peasant is the *shekinah* (the "dwelling presence") of God.[63]

For most Christians, the realities of their daily lives (their *cotidiano*) cry out in hope for radical[64] transformations; yet, arguably, their realities more often cry out for the effective empowerment of their own struggles and efforts—struggles and efforts that need to effectively transform our world's daily reality into a new *cotidiano* built on justice, on equality, on compassion, and on dignity. Put differently, most Christians hope that God will give them effective power to fight for a new reality, for them and their world. They hope that somehow, *through their struggle, with God's help,* a new world will rise. They cry out for the empowering God who will stand and fight *with* them. They trust that the hope God raised in them will become reality, as they trust that God continues to *be with* and *walk with* them—as the empowering, accompanying, and sustaining divine *shekinah.*

This hope is born from real experiences of vulnerability and need. This hope is born from their living in faith as response to the message of and about Jesus the peasant. This hope is given expression through the meanings of the terms *ruach, pneuma,* and *parakletos.* This hope leads them to understand that God is *ruach, pneuma,* and *parakletos,* as God is *equally* present in a "vulnerable peasant" like them, and who is with and sustains them (as *shekinah*).

---

[63] John 1:14. Later christological reflection will not only affirm that in this peasant God dwells, but that this peasant is the very presence of God.

[64] "Radical" is the adjective derived from the Latin noun *radix,* meaning "root." It is in the sense of a complete transformation, from the roots up, that I use the adjective.

Can or does the Mystery we call "God" be fully understood or be coextensive with human expressions, such as the above? Of course not. Can we "say" *our* experience of the Mystery we call "God" through human expressions? We have no other means, as long as it is clear that we do not equate "expression" exclusively with conceptualizing speech, because speech and concepts are not the only culturally possible ways to express ourselves. No spoken expression or concept can claim more than the non-spoken and symbolic.

When we use the expression "Holy Spirit" we refer to God—more specifically to one of the three *hypostaseis* who are the one God, in Christian trinitarian belief. When the Hebrew Scriptures use *ruach* in reference to God, or as coming from God, it is to point to divine action, to divine power and strength, to divine inspiration, to divine empowering, to divine bestowing of wisdom. When the New Testament employs *pneuma* it is referring to the *ruach* of biblical Israel and also to the divine empowering gift that marks the dawn of the new world, i.e., of the "reign*ing*" of God announced and initiated by Jesus. Consequently, the Holy Spirit is present in Jesus, in his message and life, in his death and resurrection, in his empowering. And because of this, the Spirit is also the *parakletos* on our behalf, who sustains and empowers us to follow Jesus in our lives, committed to the transformation of this world into the radically different one, willed by God, where God "reigns." God, trinitarily speaking, is creator, re-creator, and trans-creator. The Holy Spirit, as *ruach, pneuma,* and *parakletos,* is God who empowers creation, redeeming creation by building through creation (i.e., through us) the definitive "reigning of God" in creation.

Although arguably implicit in the New Testament, the Christian doctrines referring to the Holy Spirit, and the trinitarian relations in God, did not become explicit until later. I think, also, that much of what western European Christian theologians came in later centuries to discuss under the name of "grace" is often a discussion of God's "empowering" *hypostasis*—i.e., the Holy Spirit. It seems, however, that early liturgical and devotional practices had the greatest impact on what came to be said of the Holy Spirit doctrinally.

Faith and prayer preceded doctrine.[65] They preceded what came to be understood and experienced in the daily lives and daily struggles of most of the People who are the Church. Not

---

[65] For a summary of the historical developments, and current understandings, of pneumatological doctrines, within the context of trinitarian doctrinal reflections and creedal formulations, see Philip J. Rosato, "Holy Spirit," in *The Westminster Dictionary of Christian Theology*, ed. Alan Richardson and John Bowden (Philadelphia: Westminster, 1983), 262–269 and Robert P. Imbelli, Holy Spirit," in *New Dictionary of Theology*, ed. Joseph Komonchak, Mary Collins, and Dermot Lane (Wilmington, DE: Michael Glazier, 1987), 474–489. And of course, the masterful three-volume work by Yves Congar, *I Believe in the Holy Spirit* (New York: Seabury, 1983). Also, indispensably, see Carmen Nanko-Fernández, "From *Pájaro* to Paraclete: Retrieving the Spirit of God in the Company of Mary," in *Building Bridges, Doing Justice: Constructing a Latino/a Ecumenical Theology*, ed. Orlando Espín (Maryknoll, NY: Orbis, 2009), 13–28; Victor Codina, *Creo en el Espíritu Santo. Pneumatología narrativa* (Santander: Sal Terrae, 1994); Jürgen Moltmann, *The Spirit of Life: A Universal Affirmation* (Minneapolis: Fortress, 2001); José Comblin, *El Espíritu Santo y la liberación* (Madrid: Ed. Paulinas, 1987); Comblin, "The Holy Spirit," in *Mysterium Liberationis: Fundamental Concepts in Liberation Theology*, ed. Ignacio Ellacuría and Jon Sobrino (Maryknoll, NY: Orbis, 1993), 462–481; Leonardo Boff, "Trinity," in *Mysterium Liberationis*, 389–403; and Boff, *Gracia y experiencia humana* (Madrid: Trotta, 2001).

because orthodox, "learned" doctrinal statements were necessarily urgent or important for the People, but because seeking, hoping for, and expressing God's empowerment of and in their struggles was. Because the People's hope in a new world according to God's compassionate will was (and is!) the most urgent need.

Whatever the theologians and bishops say the Spirit of God is and does, seems to be—for the People—less important than the urgency of what God *actually does* in their real daily lives. Real daily life, and the empowering actions of God in it, are expressed by the People in ways often different from the spoken or written expressions of the "pious and learned."[66]

To talk of the Holy Spirit is also (but evidently not exclusively) to talk about God's power[67]—or more precisely, to talk about God's *empowerment* of the disposables of the world. To talk of the Spirit of God is to talk of God's empowerment of the human multitudes whom the world's dominant regard, and have regarded, as insignificant (to them) and thus disposable (by them). To believe in the Holy Spirit is to believe that God empowers the marginalized so that *they* may construct (with God, and in response to God) a new world of justice and equality for them and for all. The dominant's "power" is really a passing, false idol.[68]

---

[66] In this regard, see again Nanko-Fernández, "From *Pájaro* to Paraclete."

[67] Which led me to indicate above that much of what the Christian world has written about grace has to do with pneumatology, and specifically the western Christian world (probably because of Augustine's influence). A similar point is made by Leonardo Boff, *Gracia y liberación del hombre* (Madrid: Ed. Cristiandad, 1980); and Boff, *Gracia y experiencia humana*.

[68] See Luke 1:46–55.

God empowers the disposables, making them "see truth-fully" that one Jewish peasant was the self-donation (and the self-revelation) of God—a marginal "disposable" in the eyes of the powerful, but the presence of God for many of the abused. Only God's power is true and permanent. God's power empowering the disposables of Earth—*this is* the Holy Spirit.[69] Furthermore, the empowerment that is from God only occurs in *lo cotidiano*, in real daily life (i.e., incarnationally) and, there-fore, only in and through culture and the cultural.[70]

Contemporary pneumatologies, aware of the roles of human cultures and other contextualizations in human meaning constructions and truth claims,[71] must acknowledge that the ancient Christian terminologies and categories—however traditional and useful in expressing faith and doctrine in the Holy Spirit—do not and *cannot* exhaust what or who the Spirit of God is, or exhaust what may be expressed about the Spirit. And not just because it is evident that the human can never fully, sufficiently, or adequately express or under-stand the Mystery. Christian "God-talk"—especially one that

---

[69] See Comblin, *El Espíritu Santo y la liberación*.

[70] And consequently, non-innocently. And a pertinent aside: I wonder if the attraction of many Latinoax and Latin Americans to Pentecostal/Charismatic experience might not be also related to the need to *experience* "empowerment" (given their daily, seemingly powerless realities). But I think it important to ask them and to ask ourselves: Experience empowerment for what? For their/our indi-vidual "spiritual," "consoling" benefit? For their/our "feeling" close to God? The Spirit's power is deeper, and immensely more socially subversive, than the doctrinal explanations and pieties that often seem to want to "de-claw" the Spirit's world-transforming power.

[71] See Espín, *Grace and Humanness*, 51–79.

has become terminologically customary over the centuries—may be tempted to domesticate the Mystery and/or to worship itself. It may also tend to the cultural colonization of other human "God-talks"—including other Christian ones—when these dare to question the dominant God-talk terminology's pretensions as the only orthodox one possible.[72]

Consequently, the Hellenic *pneuma, parakletos*, and *hypostasis*, and the Hebrew *ruach* and *shekinah*, cannot become linguistic idols as if no other culture, terminology, symbol, or cultural construct could express, through other culturally authentic means, real (and equally "orthodox") faith in and experience of the Holy Spirit trinitarian relations.[73] In Latinoax cultures, the most "empowering" experiences and relationships are the familial and, emphatically, the maternal.[74]

The *Filioque* was once needed in the Latin West, because the Greek *ekporeuomai* was earlier thought in the Hellenic East to be self-evident to "all"—as "all" was non-innocently understood in late eastern Mediterranean antiquity's cultural and historical contexts. Nothing is ever context-free, and so

---

[72] See Espín, *Idol and Grace*, 77–84. It is indispensable to refer to Rubén Rosario Rodríguez's *Racism and God-Talk: A Latino/a Perspective* (New York: NYU Press, 2008).

[73] See Luis Pedraja, *Jesus Is My Uncle: Christology from a Hispanic Perspective* (Nashville: Abingdon, 1999), 73. Pedraja, before most, developed a similar argument in his very good, incisive, and culturally aware christology.

[74] As long as we understand that some frequent meanings of "mother," "grandmother," and "family" in the European-American world are not coextensive with *madre, abuela*, and *familia* in Latinoax contexts. There are evident similarities and coincidences, yes, but much that is crucial is still different in emphases, assumptions, expectations, intensity, and relations.

everything can be re-contextualized—thereby disrupting the dominant's cultural self-idolatries.

Philosopher John D. Caputo once wrote: "Orthodoxy is idolatry if it means holding the 'correct opinions about God' ... but not if it means holding faith in the right way, that is, not holding it at all but being held by God, in love and service."[75] It is evident that doctrinal statements could never be more than what *we* say regarding God, revelation, and human realities. However, Caputo's point is relevant regarding theology, because faith, shared prayer, spirituality, and (emphatically) solidarious service of neighbor are what should lead to theology, besides human experience and hope. Theology is *not* "books talking with books," but human reason trying to understand human reality in the light of God—but understanding it with a clearly *subversive* purpose: the transformation of that human reality into a new world of justice and compassionate solidarity (certainly, therefore, not understanding for its own sake or for a "churchy" purpose).

The Non-Innocence of
All Pneumatological Expressions

Latinoax have assumed some pneumatological expressions imported from, or imposed by, others. Given the history and dynamics of colonization, racism, and power asymmetries, this is explainable. But Latinoax have also crafted, and continue to craft, their own culturally authentic pneumatological expressions—as orthodox and as frail as those imposed on them by others.

---

[75] John D. Caputo, *What Would Jesus Deconstruct?: The Good News of Postmodernism for the Church* (Grand Rapids: Baker Academic, 2007), 131.

Christians have become traditionally accustomed to employing the terms "Father," "Son," and "Holy Spirit," while often not noticing how human, cultural, and androcentric these terms are and have always been. We do not think of how analogically limited these terms are and can only be or of how they do not, and cannot, fully express the Ineffable Mystery Christians call "God." Human words, no matter how wonderfully true we might hold them to be, only and always remain human words. Only and always! They might sacramentally, symbolically, or analogically state what *we* believe God has revealed about Godself, but our words are not God or God's, or capable of "explaining" God.[76]

We should recall, as I have already indicated, that ecclesial and doctrinal understandings and affirmations about Jesus have frequently stripped him of his Jewish roots and of his cultural/historical/social realities, and this has often led to disincarnate christological affirmations—i.e., void of any real human dimension.[77] The real-life, rural, landless, poor Jewish Jesus is made unnecessary, irrelevant, and/or effectively denied.

Christianity, therefore, cannot deny or hide the human flesh in the Incarnation, make it irrelevant, or, even unintentionally,

---

[76] To think otherwise is idolatrous.

[77] See J. Kameron Carter, *Race: A Theological Account* (Oxford: Oxford University Press, 2008). Docetism remains a real temptation to Christian understandings of Jesus and, therefore, of revelation. Docetism (as Carter and others suggest) is arguably the probable ground on which a "white, Eurocentric" Jesus and Christianity came to be. See also Rosemary P. Carbine, "Docetism," in *Introductory Dictionary of Theology and Religious Studies*, 359–360. My thanks to my former student Tarez Lemmons for raising several important questions that led to my reflection on these issues.

dismiss or marginalize the biblical and early Christian witness. Stripping Jesus of his Jewishness and of his poverty is the source of the (intentional or not, but nevertheless real) historical ideological manipulation that made Jesus white and stripped his core message of its indisputable socially subversive content in exchange for an other-worldly paradise for individuals' souls.[78]

Historical contexts and means are crucial for the interpretation of doctrines, but they cannot be held to be coextensive with the "affirmation" or "insight" the linguistic, cultural, historical expressions intended to convey. A doctrine may (and often does) convey *more* than the architects of the doctrine—in and through their cultural, linguistic, historical contexts—could understand and express, because theirs are not the only contexts or the only understandings possible of any doctrine.[79] *Incessant incarnation of the "insights" conveyed by human doctrines is indispensable*, if these intend to "say" truth within Christianity in time. But these incessant incarnations will need to reflect the faith and expressions of the "disposables" in *other* contexts, in order to claim that they "affirm" revelation and thus what may be held as true.[80] *Because* the definitive *self*-revelation of God

---

[78] I am convinced that it is impossible that Jesus of Nazareth, a Jewish peasant speaking as a peasant with other Jewish peasants in the cultural context of Galilean Jewish peasants, during Roman-occupied Palestine, would have engaged in discourse regarding the fate or immortality of souls. The mere concept of an "immortal soul" that can survive death and "go to heaven" would have been unthinkable and unsayable among Galilean Jewish peasants at the time.

[79] On this rests the very notion and possibility of a history and development of doctrines.

[80] Indispensable in this conversation, of course, is Latin America's liberation theology and its well-argued insistence on the role

occurred in and as a "disposable" peasant, who addressed other "disposables," who gave birth to Christianity as a subversive community of "disposables" committed to the transformation of *this* world according to God's will.[81]

Doctrines "affirm" something. There is a "content," an "insight," conveyed through any doctrine's linguistic, cultural medium; but that "insight" or "affirmation" is not reducible to the doctrinal statement or claim, or to its linguistic and conceptual means. Nor can any doctrine (as expression of an "insight" deemed necessary in Christianity) claim that it is the perfect, complete and only possible expression. If an "insight" deemed necessary by Christians cannot be incarnate and expressed in and through the means authentic to *any other* cultural context, then the "insight" is denied under the guise of being orthodox.[82] Self-colonizing repetition is not orthodoxy.

European/Mediterranean contexts, past and present, expressed the pneumatological through European/Mediterranean linguistic, cultural, and historical means. This was and is inevitable. But Europeans also *colonially* exported and

---

of the poor. I remind the reader of the works by Gustavo Gutiérrez, Leonardo Boff, Ignacio Ellacuría, Juan Luis Segundo, Jon Sobrino, Segundo Galilea, Lucio Gera, Juan C. Scannone, José Comblin, Ricardo Antoncich, João Batista Libânio, Ivone Gebara, Carlos Mesters, Paulo F. Carneiro de Andrade, Maria Clara Bingemer, and many others. Also important to the conversation are the final documents of the Latin American bishops' conferences held in Medellín (1968) and Puebla (1979).

[81] See Espín, *Idol and Grace*, 1–13, 77–130.

[82] Karl Rahner suggested that merely or mainly repeating dogma, without interpretation in context, will eventually become heresy. See Karl Rahner, "Thoughts on the Possibility of Belief Today," in *Theological Investigations*, vol. 5 (New York: Crossroad, 1983).

imposed these same (inescapably contextualized and limited) doctrines on others (of different linguistic, cultural, historical contexts) as *the* "correct" and *the* "invariable" expressions of *the* "truth." But what could the colonized have understood (what *did* they "receive") regarding the "Spirit of God," and "Trinity," in the violent contexts of conquest and colonization, within colonization's violent and inescapable power asymmetries, and the European (white) hegemonic and violent imposition of racism, slavery, and economic dominance, also as "truth" and "revealed" (or at least morally permitted) by God?[83]

The pneumatological "sayings" from the Latinoax (and Latin American) contexts—which are historical and cultural heirs of the victims of conquest and bigotry—should be understood as indispensable hermeneutic, because (among many other ethical and doctrinal reasons) Christianity cannot disregard or downplay the horrors inflicted in its name or the "disposable" social location of Jesus of Nazareth. If Jesus *is* the *self*-revelation of God, then those "disposable" like Jesus cannot be ignored or marginalized (in any generation or context) when it comes to "saying" the pneumatological correctly and "truth-fully."[84] There is no Christianity without a crucified, "disposable" peasant at its claimed origin.[85] There is no

---

[83] See Orlando Espín, "Trinitarian Monotheism and the Birth of Popular Catholicism: The Case of Sixteenth-Century Mexico," *Missiology*, 20:2 (1992): 177–204. This article analyzes the reasons why the proclamation and acceptance of trinitarian monotheism were extremely difficult outside of Europe, especially in and because of sixteenth- and seventeenth-century contexts of violence and colonization imposed on others by "Christian" Europe.

[84] See Carter, *Race*.

[85] The crucifixion of Jesus was socially possible and acceptable

Christianity, furthermore, where the "disposables" of subsequent generations and contexts are unheard, dismissed, or further victimized by those who might claim to be Christian.[86] Power and social asymmetries are not innocent—as non-innocent as the doctrinal "sayings" of the hegemonic when *they* declare *their* "sayings" as the only ones acceptable as "correct" doctrine.

The Empowering Spirit

The "empowering Spirit" is not just a term or expression, even if we can only use limited and limiting human words and symbols to refer to God. Christian history arrived at terms and symbols employed in pneumatology because of the *empowering experiences* (again, lived faith preceding doctrine) that led Christians to see and understand that what was deemed impossible has or can become possible thanks to *God's empowerment of us*. The chosen terms and symbols should point to and unveil (before and above all else) the *experiences* of empowerment—of God's making possible for us to discover that *we can* do, *we can* become, *we can* transform.[87]

---

by his "disposable" socio-economic status in Roman-occupied Jewish Palestine's context of power asymmetries and military violence.

[86] Pope Francis: "To ignore the poor is to scorn God." See Francis's reflection on the parable in Luke 16: 19–31, at his General Audience (Rome), May 18, 2016: https://www.vatican.va/content/francesco/en/audiences/2016/documents/papa-francesco_20160518_udienza-generale.html.

[87] See Exod. 3:7–12, esp. v. 12. The point that *the "proof" of God's empowerment is the human doing what would have been regarded as impossible* is a crucially grounding theme in Exodus, repeated in other biblical texts and in the history of Christian spirituality. "Success,"

But never has any pneumatological term or symbol been adopted, or will any ever be adopted, and employed without somehow reflecting the power asymmetries and other realities of its cultural (birthing and/or adoptive) contexts. In this sense, *madre* and *abuela* are as apt, for pneumatological use, as the earlier Hebrew or Hellenic terms. And they are just as non-innocent, and unequal. We cannot forget that Latinoax mothers, grandmothers, and families do not have the same respect, rights, and importance as white mothers, grandmothers or, families have in a society built on structures of normalized white privilege justified by Eurocentric assumptions of (white) cultural superiority.

The New Testament gospels introduced the symbolic use of a dove into the Christian imaginary to refer to the empowering presence of the Spirit of God.[88] The apparently gentle and vulnerable dove appears as the most frequent gospel symbol of the Spirit's empowering of *Jesus's* mission and defiance. Other symbols (flames, earth tremors, unexpected occurrences) seem more frequently related to the Spirit's empowerment of the *disciples'* mission. Despite later artistic preferences, the early Christian symbolic choices to refer to the Holy Spirit were not limited to a few. The symbols

---

however, is not the point. Rather, what is underlined is that *active trust in and commitment to living according to God's will* (i.e., to do and be as God wills, which is made possible by God's empowerment) *will turn the hoped-for impossible into the real and possible.* Consequently, only those human actions that help transform this world into the new world of compassionate solidarity, willed by God, can be seen as expressing God's will and empowerment—and therefore, only these are truly pneumatological. See Espín, *Idol and Grace*, 1–7.

[88] See Matt. 3:16; Mark 1:10; Luke 3:22; John 1:32; etc.

employed to affirm the pneumatological were "action markers" that intended to identify or interpret the Spirit's empowering presence. Any symbol for the Holy Spirit, therefore, would (crucially) need to be understood as a *marker of the Spirit's empowering action.*[89]

All empowering actions of the Spirit—to the degree that they are understood by humans, and to the degree that humans are affected by the Spirit's actions—happen in time, and in human social and cultural contexts. The human creation or adoption of a symbol for the empowering actions of the Spirit, "marking" the Spirit's subversive presence, requires human intelligibility of the symbolized empowering action and of the symbol that points to it. But *because*—in Christian belief and hope—no empowering act of the Holy Spirit enslaves, demeans, or falsifies the human, the symbols adopted cannot do or foster these either. The Spirit liberates and humanizes. Furthermore and consequently, the symbols for the pneumatological must be culturally authentic, while being equally

---

[89] That is why the traditional "gifts of the Spirit" may also be better understood as "markers of the Spirit's empowering action" in ecclesial communities and in human societies, seeking and provoking the transformation of all into the new, shared and solidarious world God wills. The traditional list of the Spirit's "seven gifts" (i.e., wisdom, understanding, counsel, fortitude, knowledge, piety, and fear of the Lord) is a list too prone to be understood as individual gifts for individual spiritual benefit, without necessarily provoking communal behaviors that subvert the religious, social, and cultural *status quo.* Unfortunately, this is a list (culturally, socially, and ecclesially) easily "tamed." Reason enough to wonder if it really (or sufficiently) expresses the world-subversive "gifts" of the same Spirit of God who sustained Jesus' defiance of his *status quo.*

subversive of their birthing culture's *status quo*. "Incarnation" is the theological term that perhaps best states the needed, real cultural authenticity that carries with and in itself the provocation and means to subvert the world as it is.[90]

Most pneumatological terms and symbols, in white-privileging US society and culture, as well as among the majority of Christians throughout Christian history (especially after the fifteenth-century European conquest, colonization, and enslavement of the majority others), have been misunderstood or manipulated.

Dominant "Christian" societies have misunderstood *the defiance of the symbolic dove*—i.e., that something so vulnerable and weak and easily controlled was in fact symbolizing

---

[90] Regarding the culturally and socially subversive thrust of real pneumatological experiences, symbols and terms, I earlier referred to Comblin's *El Espíritu Santo y la liberación*, esp. 74–94; but also see José Comblin, *O Espírito no mundo* (Petrópolis: Vozes, 1978). I have already referred to Boff's *Gracia y liberación del hombre* and his *Gracia y experiencia humana*, and also to Díaz, *On Being Human*. Important in this regard are Medina, "Theological Musings toward a Latinoax Pneumatology," in *Wiley-Blackwell Companion to Latinoax Theology*, 173–190; Roberto S. Goizueta, "Grace, Sin, and Salvation," in *Wiley-Blackwell Companion to Latinoax Theology*, 215–230; Piet Fransen, "Desarrollo histórico de la doctrina de la gracia," in *Mysterium Saluti*, ed. J. Feiner and M. Löhrer, (Madrid: Cristiandad, 1969), IV/2:611–730; Rahner, *Foundations of Christian Faith*; Rahner, "Gracia: exposición teológica," in *Sacramentum Mundi 3*:319–334; Orlando Espín, "Grace and Humanness: A Hispanic Perspective," in Roberto S. Goizueta, *We Are a People!: Initiatives in Hispanic American Theology* (Minneapolis: Fortress, 1992), 133–164; and Martin Gelabert Ballester, *Salvación como humanización: Esbozo de una teología de la gracia* (Madrid: Paulinas, 1985).

the subversive (divine) power behind the dawn of the "Reign of God," and the subsequent demise of human hegemonies.[91]

No society or culture exists without "convincing" most of its population (while hiding from them the processes employed in the convincing) that they should be "led"—and hence, be marginalized from the "mainstream" established by those with the power to convince. No society exists, therefore, without the dynamics, decisions, conflicts, manipulations, and interests that have been bundled under the label "hegemony."[92]

All of the above is important for pneumatology. Because if the Spirit of God is the divine empowerer who makes possible the construction of the "Reign of God" in this world, then the

---

[91]   See Luke 1:46–55, and Luke 6:20–26.

[92]   In the Gramscian sense of the term. See Antonio Gramsci, *Os Intelectuais e a Organização da Cultura* [trans. of *Gli intelletuali e l'organizzazione della cultura*] (Rio de Janeiro: Ed. Civilização Brasileira, 1979) and Gramsci's other works referred to earlier in this chapter. See also Portelli, *Gramsci et le bloc historique*; Gruppi, *O conceito de hegemonia em Gramsci*; Neil Pearson, *Antonio Gramsci: The Concept of 'Hegemony'* (2014, P Publishing International Relations Series; only in Kindle edition); and Carlos N. Coutinho, "O conceito de vontade coletiva em Gramsci," *Katálysis* 12, no. 1 (2009), http://www.scielo. br/. Although I do not completely agree with his reading of Gramsci, I found Coutinho's text very suggestive. See also Kevin Thompson, "Religion, Values, and Ideology," in *Modernity: An Introduction to Modern Societies*, ed. Stuart Hall et al. (Malden, MA: Wiley-Blackwell, 1996), 395–422, esp. 410–412. I also referred earlier in this chapter to the work of Ernesto Laclau regarding hegemony. Pertinent here and in what follows are Slavoj Zizek, *The Sublime Object of Ideology* (London: Verso, 2008 [first ed. 1989]) and especially Zizek, *The Parallax View* (Cambridge, MA: MIT Press, 2009), 37–67 and 330–385. Laclau's understanding of hegemony is also the focus of Zizek's interest.

Spirit of God has evidently "taken sides" in the contexts and conflicts of hegemony.

If a radically new world is needed and inevitably coming—as Christians must centrally claim as *God's will* expressed by *the core message* of Jesus—then the only logical conclusion is that the current world is *not* according to God's will. But, of course, this is not "good news" for the beneficiaries of the current world.[93] More importantly, what has been said throughout twenty centuries of Christianity regarding the Spirit of God—i.e., all of pneumatology's creedal and theological constructs—cannot oppose, dismiss, or be interpreted to oppose or dismiss the aforementioned logical conclusion.

Within Christian theology it must be clear: the Spirit of God has taken sides in favor of those for whom a new world of justice, solidarity, equality, and compassion would really be "good news"—in other words, God has taken the side of those who would most benefit from the "reigning of God."[94]

---

[93] See Espín, *Idol and Grace*, 1–7, 84–129.

[94] I remind the reader that there can be no Christianity or Christian theology without Jesus of Nazareth. We must further remember that the "Reign" or "reigning" of God—with all that it subversively implied—was claimed by the earliest Christians to be the core message of Jesus of Nazareth. Then, by which doctrinal or theological argument could some pretend to do "serious, rigorous theology" if it implies dismissing and "de-clawing" the core message of Jesus?

2

Pentecost at Tepeyac?

"In the name of the Father, and of the Son, and of ... Whom?"

I have suggested before that the *Virgen de Guadalupe* may be understood in other than the typical "Marian" terms.[1] But before

---

[1] I have written on Guadalupe before: See Orlando Espín, *The Faith of the People: Theological Reflections on Popular Catholicism* (Maryknoll, NY: Orbis, 1997); Espín, "An Exploration Into the Theology of Grace and Sin," in *From the Heart of Our People*, ed. Orlando Espín and Miguel H. Díaz (Maryknoll, NY: Orbis, 1999), 121–152; Espín, "The Vanquished, Faithful Solidarity and the Marian Symbol: A Hispanic Perspective on Providence," in *On Keeping Providence*, ed. Barbara Doherty and Joan Coultas (Terre Haute, IN: St. Mary of the Woods College Press, 1991), 84–101; Espín, "Mary in Latino/a Catholicism: Four Types of Devotion," *New Theological Review* 23, no. 3 (2010): 16–25; and my unpublished 2004 Bellarmine Lecture at Loyola Marymount University, "The Virgin of Guadalupe and the Holy Spirit: A Mexican and Mexican American Understanding of the Divine." Much has been written by other scholars on the *Virgen de Guadalupe* and the devotion to her. For example, see Stafford Poole, *Our Lady of Guadalupe: The Origins and Sources of a Mexican National Symbol, 1531–1797* (Tucson: University of Arizona Press, 1995); Virgilio Elizondo and Timothy Matovina, eds.,

proceeding, we need to ask how Latinoax understand and represent God *latinamente*. This is not as easy as it might seem.

As peoples who have been marginalized by dominant society, Latinoax have culturally introjected many of the ideas and "images" about God proposed by those who are dominant in Church and society. Indeed, part of the dynamics of marginalization is that the marginalized are bombarded with, and are *partially* convinced by, the arguments and reasons of the dominant.[2] So, if we were to ask Latinoax about God, we would hear much of what we could hear from others in the wider Church and society. Because most Latinoax are Catholic, their repetition of many of these ideas and representations is and will be due to their Catholicism. But although this seems to be true, it is also just as true that Latinoax are Latinoax; and therefore their introjection and expressions of doctrines and representations of the Divine is still *a culturally Latinoax process*. This does not make them "less Catholic" (or Catholic in a suspect way) than it did the Irish, the German, the Iberian, or the (Patristic period) Hellenic.[3]

New Frontiers in Guadalupan Studies (Eugene, OR: Wipf and Stock, 2014); and Jeanette Rodríguez, *Our Lady of Guadalupe: Faith and Empowerment among Mexican-American Women* (Austin: University of Texas Press, 1994). Indispensable is María Del Socorro Castañeda, *Our Lady of Everyday Life: La Virgen de Guadalupe and the Catholic Imagination of Mexican Women in America* (New York: Oxford University Press, 2018).

[2] Antonio Gramsci is again my guide here, especially his understanding and analyses of "hegemony" and of the subaltern's "doubts" within the "historical bloc." I have, in chap. 1, included bibliographic references to Gramsci's thought on these particulars.

[3] A fascinating scholarly contribution is Cecilia Titizano, "*Mama*

In other words, the very Catholic identity of Latinoax does not cancel or diminish their cultural "lenses" and identity, but rather *must* make Latinoax Catholics be Catholic *latinamente*. There is no *a*-cultural Christianity, ever! And thus, if Latinoax are Catholic (and the majority of us are) then we must be so *latinamente*, or we are not Catholic. Consequently, if we are to experience, understand and "image" God as Catholics, Latinoax must do so *latinamente*.[4] There is no alternative … except to (intentionally or misguidedly) confuse the theologically or pastorally "correct" with the colonization (or, worse, the self-colonization) of Latinoax Catholics. On the one hand, because most Latinoax *are Catholic*,[5] they must somehow experience, understand, and "image" the Divine in ways that, although culturally specific, must be legitimately identifiable as Christian. On the other hand, because Latinoax Catholics *are Latinoax*, they also have to be able to experience, understand, and "image" the Divine in ways that, although identifiably Christian, must also be identifiable as culturally Latinoax. There is no escaping this dual need. Furthermore, the definers

---

Pacha: Creator and Sustainer Spirit of God," *Horizontes Decoloniales* 3 (2017): 127–159. Titizano accomplishes an important pneumatological hermeneutic of the Andean *Mama Pacha*.

[4] I want to suggest that, pastorally *and* theologically, this is crucial to Catholicism in the US. The future will not tolerate or allow US (and worldwide) Catholicism to ignore its demographic, culturally diverse reality. The future of Catholicism in the US is, indisputably, Latinoax—unless the institutions of the US Church continue to downplay the importance of our cultural identities and traditions.

[5] It is indispensable that we do not confuse faith with the observance of ecclesiastical laws and regulations. Faith life and church laws are not coextensive or mutually necessary.

of what is Latinoax are the Latinoax, just as the definers of what is Catholic are the Catholics—but remembering the fact that the majority of Catholics in the US are Latinoax, and that (because the Church *is* the People) the majority of Catholics in the world are not Europeans or Eurocentric whites.

But has the Divine been imaged *latinamente*? How have Latinoax done it, while still marginalized by the dominant in Church and society, with all that this marginalization implies and has historically implied? It seems to me that we may have to legitimately and reasonably ask whether some *apparently* Marian devotions might not in fact be both Latinoax culturally specific and fully Christian representations *of God*,[6] and more concretely, of the Holy Spirit.

Let me clarify what I am *not* saying.

1. I am not suggesting or implying that Mary, the mother of Jesus, is God or divine, in any way, for Latinoax Catholics. This claim would be outright unacceptable to any Catholic and, thus, unacceptable to Latinoax Catholics as well.

2. I am not implying, or leading to the conclusion, that Latinoax Catholics are insufficiently evangelized because of what they may be implicitly assuming and expressing about or through some *apparently* Marian devotions.

---

[6] "The only true representation is one that also represents its distance from the truth." I am not suggesting otherwise here or anywhere else. The quoted phrase is from Giorgio Agamben, *Idea of Prose* (Albany, NY: SUNY Press, 1995), 107.

3. I am not saying that Latinoax Catholics have somehow fallen into a form of syncretism if and when they represent God through a Marian symbol.[7]

4. I am not assuming or saying that every Latinoax Catholic (in order to be really Latinoax and really Catholic) has necessarily to represent the Divine through symbols customarily associated with Mary—there is nothing genetic about this, and obviously there are many authentically Latinoax Catholics who do not represent God through a Marian symbol. "*A* culturally authentic" expression is not equal to "*the* culturally authentic" expression.

Symbols used to speak of or represent Mary are as cultural, perspectival, and limited as the symbols of "father," "son," *pneuma*, *ruach*, *parakletos*, tongue of fire, and dove, when used to speak of or represent God. And like these, the symbols used in relation to Mary are not and cannot be exhausted by specific interpretations within specific historical and cultural contexts.

---

[7] All symbols can be re-interpreted, as Caputo has insisted, if their contextualizations change. Or, as Derrida has suggested, all "texts" have surpluses of meanings, thus making it impossible for one usage or interpretation (of a text or a symbol) to be the only usage or interpretation possible. See John D. Caputo, *Truth: Philosophy in Transit* (New York: Penguin Books, 2013) and Jacques Derrida, *Margins of Philosophy* (Chicago: University of Chicago Press, 1982). I remind the reader of my earlier discussions of symbols and their roles in conflictual, asymmetric societies, and the bibliography cited there. We will return to this discussion.

What Do Catholics Believe
Regarding the Holy Spirit?

Catholics believe:

1. That the Holy Spirit is one of the three "ways" in which the one God is eternally God, in the triune Ineffable Mystery.
2. That the Holy Spirit is loving, accepting, sustaining, guiding, and correcting.
3. That the Holy Spirit leads and comforts, teaches, counsels and enlightens, encourages and empowers, makes possible faith, hope, and solidarious love.

Although many Catholics throughout the world have not seemed particularly adept at employing explicit "pneumatological" doctrinal language, it is undeniable that any real ("popular" or "learned") understanding of Catholic doctrine, liturgy, and devotional practice will easily discover the presence, belief in, and action of the Holy Spirit throughout the Catholic tradition's universe.

There are historical reasons for the apparent Catholic paucity of explicit pneumatological language, but paucity of explicit language about something does not equal absence or misunderstanding of that which the explicit language might name. The key question to raise, again, is *not* whether among Latinoax Catholics there is explicit pneumatological language used in reference to Mary but, rather, whether Latinoax *relate with the Holy Spirit through transferred and reinterpreted symbols that originated in the universe of Marian devotions.* We must remember that *relationship* is the grounding key component of and in any devotion.

The reader should wonder how many Catholics today (and how many in the Church's ordained leadership) would feel comfortable talking about and relating to God in the feminine.[8] The usual reaction of many (most?) Catholics is that if something is feminine, it must relate to Mary, because if it relates to God it has to be masculine; somehow they do not see the inconsistency between this and the necessary Christian belief that God is beyond all our categories and genders. All language about God, Catholics would correctly say, is a cultural construct. Language about God is not God. And that is precisely my point. As Augustine of Hippo insightfully said, *si comprehendis, non est Deus.*[9]

Consequently, and as I have been explaining in the present volume, in Catholic belief and piety it *must* be admissible and expected—and this should not surprise us—that diverse cultural human groups can express, "translate," and "image" God in diverse manners authentic within their respective cultural contexts. In fact, many Latinoax seem sometimes to *relate* with/to "Mary" as if she were divine—perhaps indicating a deeper pneumatological, Trinitarian faith than most *non*-Latinoax are ready to acknowledge. Life is stronger than words, and Latinoax life seems to be clearly and insistently suggesting that Marian symbols often represent the "pneumatological" (i.e., the Holy Spirit) among Latinoax.[10]

---

[8] See Leonardo Boff, *A Ave-María. O Feminino e o Espíritu Santo* (Petrópolis: Ed. Vozes, 2014).

[9] "If you can comprehend (understand) it, it isn't God." Augustine of Hippo, *Sermo* 117.3.5 (ca. 418 CE).

[10] I must again remind the reader that *all* symbols can be re-interpreted, and all texts have surpluses of meanings, thus making it impossible for one usage or interpretation (of a text or a symbol)

Can God be expressed and "imaged" among Latinoax Catholics through their borrowing of Marian symbols and terminology? Can Latinoax "say God" (knowing full well that all language about God cannot "capture" or fully express the Divine) through symbols, practices, and language borrowed from their Marian devotions, just as Europeans, over many centuries, spoke of and "imaged" God in monarchical, patriarchal, racial, androcentric, and even tribal terms? The answer to these questions is, simply and clearly, an emphatic "yes!"[11]

Consequently, we must further ask:

1. Who, in Latinoax cultures, is the frequent image and symbol of loving, accepting, sustaining, guiding, empowering, and correcting?
2. Who, in Latinoax cultures, leads and comforts, teaches, counsels and enlightens, gives courage, and makes possible faith, hope, and love?

Many Latinoax would answer both questions by recalling their relationship with their mothers and grandmothers.[12]

---

to be the only usage or interpretation possible. See Caputo, *Truth: Philosophy in Transit* and Derrida, *Margins of Philosophy.*

[11] Latino Pentecostal theologian Néstor Medina has written an important study on the ecumenical possibilities of re-thinking Mary and pneumatology. See Néstor Medina, "Unlikely Siblings? Pentecostal Ethico-Theological Insights from Catholic Teaching on Mary" in *Receptive Ecumenism as Transformative Ecclesial Learning: Walking the Way to a Church Re-Formed*, ed. Paul Murray, Gregory Ryan, and Paul Lakeland (Oxford: Oxford University Press, 2022), 263–274.

[12] Obviously, not all Latinoax mothers and grandmothers are (or could be) described thus, just as not only mothers and grandmothers

Who, I then ask, within the Trinity that is God, is typically identified in orthodox Catholic belief and piety with the qualities and actions I have just mentioned? Most Catholics will correctly answer "the Holy Spirit."

If God can be referred to in "paternal" terms, then God can be referred to in "maternal" ones too.[13] As "father" carries all sorts of stereotypes and "baggage" in most human languages and societies, so does "mother," yet this should not stop us from using familial terms for the Ineffable Trinitarian Mystery—as long as we do not confuse the human words with the being of God, and as long as we remember that human words are the only words we have. After all, the Word addressed by God to us *became human in order for us to begin to understand the radical solidarity of God with us.*

Then, I propose, the symbols, language, images borrowed from Mary can be used (as all human language can and cannot be) to speak about and image the Holy Spirit and express the relationship with the Divine *latinamente*.[14] I am convinced that it is *not* the Jewish woman Mary of Nazareth, the mother of Jesus, that most Latinoax (especially Mexican Americans) speak of when they refer to the *Virgen de Guadalupe.*

---

play these roles in Latinoax families. Frequency is all I am suggesting and not gender stereotyping.

[13] See Elizabeth Johnson, "Mary and the Female Face of God, *Theological Studies* 50 (1989): 500–526.

[14] The only objection, it seems clear, would be the one arising from cultural or ecclesiastical androcentrism. This androcentric claim rests on the supposition that androcentric human language is necessary in order to correctly speak of the being of the Mystery we call "God." Such claim, however, borders on idolatry and is therefore unacceptable.

I am not satisfied with some of the alternatives offered in the past—e.g., that Guadalupe is Tonantzin, or another earth goddess, or some sort of personified syncretization between the Christian Mary and the Nahua Tonantzin,[15] or a new Marian-Nahua *mestiza* symbol invented by sixteenth-century Iberian missionaries in order to promote their evangelization efforts, and so on. These alternatives seem to assume that "symbolized" and "symbol" are univocal and univalent, regardless of time or context.

Stafford Poole's book, *Our Lady of Guadalupe: The Origins and Sources of a Mexican National Symbol,*[16] *incisively* raises a number of questions and issues for those who would study the Guadalupan devotion. His book is an important examination of the main written texts that—in colonial and independent Mexico—have served as sources employed to support or dismiss the traditional narrative of Guadalupe "apparitions," and of the devotion that preceded and followed them. Poole's cultural and methodological assumptions, however, represent a clearly dominant, Eurocentric perspective that regards as "lacking" any cultural construct not "substantiated" by the written word or the preserved artifact. I have serious objections to his methodological decision to dismiss all oral, performed, *un*written evidence as unimportant, unreliable, or unacceptable—which implies a dismissal of most of humanity's history and memory.[17]

---

[15] See Ana Castillo, ed., *Goddess of the Americas: Writings on the Virgin of Guadalupe* (New York: Riverhead, 1997). The chapters in this important volume, by various authors, reflect several prominent interpretations of Guadalupe. *Goddess of the Americas* is an indispensable resource, whether one agrees or disagrees with its several authors.

[16] See n. 1 above.

[17] Biblical scholars and scholars of historiography would probably shout the reasonable warning "Beware what you wish for!" at

Nevertheless, Poole's book does challenge the Latinoax devout (including some Latinoax theologians) to demonstrate that the *Virgen de Guadalupe* did in fact appear in 1531 on the hill of Tepeyac, or honestly and explicitly to acknowledge that they are basing much on an unsubstantiated story.[18]

We must certainly consider and admit that oral traditions exist and have always existed, and they do not merely convey "legends." But they do not merely convey facts either. Truth can be and is conveyed through myth—as biblical and other scholars continue to demonstrate—because "truth" and "real" are not reducible to what can now be measured, observed, or weighed.[19] Put differently, a prior analysis and critique needs to be done on the epistemological foundations of the dominant Eurocentric, as well as on the epistemological foundations *and* historical contexts of the (literate or illiterate) non-Eurocentric.[20]

Poole and others who seem so comfortable with the literate elites' methodological (and self-blinding) assumptions.

[18] The devotion to Guadalupe existed, in colonial Mexico, for several decades prior to the appearance of the story told by the *Nican Mopohua* (i.e., the devotion preceded the story of apparitions). The painting of the *Virgen de Guadalupe* did too.

[19] If only the now observable (etc.) were truth, humanity would be hard pressed to demonstrate the importance of its highest moral values and of humans' commitment to them as well as to defy the history of science and of scientific discoveries repeatedly debunking what had before been held as "evident" and as "fact."

[20] As I stated, Poole's book has some serious limitations and, since its publication, there have been other important publications that also need to be considered. See Maxwell E. Johnson, *The Virgin of Guadalupe: Reflections of an Anglo-Lutheran Liturgist* (Lanham, MD: Rowman and Littlefield, 2002); Elizabeth Johnson, "Mary and the Image of God," in *Mary, Woman of Nazareth: Biblical and Theological*

Stafford Poole's work made me wonder if there might not *also* be another line of thought opening for us here. He ignores (or at least does not want to take into account) that the written

Perspectives, ed. Doris Donnelly (New York: Paulist, 1987), 25–68; and Johnson, "Mary and the Female Face of God." See also the articles by Javier Traslosheros, Timothy Matovina, Michael Engh, Jeanette Rodrí-guez, and Virgilio Elizondo in the special issue on Guadalupe, *Journal of Hispanic/Latino Theology* 5, no.1 (1997); Richard Nebel, *Santa María Tonantzin Virgen de Guadalupe. Continuidad y transformación religiosa en México* (Mexico City: Fondo de Cultura Económica, 1995); Xavier Noguez, *Documentos guadalupanos. Un estudio sobre las fuentes de información tempranas en torno a las mariofanías en el Tepeyac* (Mexico City: Fondo de Cultura Económica, 1993); Casta-ñeda, *Our Lady of Everyday Life*; Ernest Burrus, *The Oldest Copy of the Nican Mopohua* (Washington, DC: CARA, 1981); Burrus, *The Basic Bibliography of the Guadalupan Apparitions, 1531–1723* (Washington, DC: CARA, 1983); Centro de Estudios Guadalupanos, *Documen-tario guadalupano, 1531–1768*, Monumenta Histórica Guadalupana Series 3 (Mexico City: Centro de Estudios Guadalupanos, 1980); Mary DeCock, "Our Lady of Guadalupe: Symbol of Liberation?" in *Mary According to Women*, ed. Carol Frances Jegen (Kansas City, MO: Leaven, 1985); Ernesto de la Torre Villar and Ramiro Navarro de Anda, *Testimonios históricos guadalupanos. Compilación, prólogo, notas bibliográficas e índices* (Mexico City: Fondo de Cultura Económica, 1982); David Kurtz, "The Virgin of Guadalupe and the Politics of Becoming Human," *Journal of Anthropological Research* 38 (1982): 194–210; Jacques Lafaye, *Quetzalcóatl and Guadalupe: The Formation of Mexican National Consciousness, 1531–1813* (Chicago: University of Chicago Press, 1987); Benjamín Bravo, ed., *Diccionario de religios-idad popular* (Mexico City: Lib. Parroquial, 1992); Mario Rojas, *Nican Mopohua. Traducción del náhuatl al castellano* (Huejutla/Mexico City: Librería Parroquial, 1978); Clodomir L. Siller Acuña, "Anotaciones y comentarios al *Nican Mopohua*," *Estudios Indígenas* 8, no. 2 (1981): 217–274; Rebecca Berrú-Davis, "Guadalupita: La Virgen Peregrina.

material from colonial Mexico on Guadalupe was *necessarily* going to promote (for theological, ecclesiastical, and political reasons) the view that the *Virgen de Guadalupe* was/is Mary of Nazareth. We cannot dismiss as unimportant the power asymmetries evident in conquered, colonial central Mexico. But *is the Virgen de Guadalupe the same as Mary?* It seems clear that literate[21] *criolloax*, as well as literate Hispanicized *mestizoax* and Natives were all enthusiastically promoting the notion that Mary had appeared in Mexico. Whatever their ultimate intentions in pushing this view, these colonial and colonized authors would have found it unacceptable (*and personally dangerous!*) to think of Guadalupe in *any* other terms. They could have been accused of crypto-paganism, of heresy, or of something to that effect, if they had expressed any doubt that Guadalupe is just another way of referring to the mother of Jesus.[22] One must also remember that during the sixteenth and seventeenth centuries (i.e., the period of the origin of the Guadalupe devotion in Mexico), western Europe was undergoing the events

An Ethnographic Study," *Perspectivas* (Fall 2009): 22–49; María J. Castro Dopacio, *Emperatriz de las Américas: La Virgen de Guadalupe en la literatura chicana* (Valencia, Spain: Universidad de Valencia, 2010); Theresa Delgadillo, *Spiritual Mestizaje: Religion, Gender, Race and Nation in Contemporary Chicana Narrative* (Durham: Duke University Press, 2011); and Patrizia Granziera, "From Coatlicue to Guadalupe: The Image of the Great Mother in Mexico," *Studies in World Christianity* 10, no. 2: 250–273.

[21] Literacy in colonial Mexico was not widespread among the population, as it also was a sign of privilege in and among Native, *mestizoax*, and *criolloax* colonial society.

[22] See Richard E. Greenleaf, "The Mexican Inquisition and the Indians: Sources for the Ethnohistorian," *The Americas* 34, no. 3 (1978): 315–344.

and doctrinal effects of the various Reformations. Within Spanish-dominated Mexico's 1500s and 1600s, consequently, it would have been interpreted as "heretical" to make any religious claim that did not plainly appear thoroughly "Catholic." Anything that *appeared* to be "Marian," therefore, would have been judged as "safe."

But, what if for *that* purpose the *criollo* clergy had to originally write "an almost forgotten narrative"[23] of the origin of the increasingly popular *Native* "devotion" to a non-Iberian Guadalupe? The equally orthodox alternative to the "Marian enthusiasm" displayed was not, and did not have to be, crypto-paganism or heresy. It could simply have been traditional Christian pneumatology. Was it or is it impossible for orthodox, traditional Christian theology to think the divine in feminine categories and images?[24] Obviously not; but, for the literate elites in colonial Mexico, maybe yes—and for potentially dangerous reasons.

Perhaps historians' and theologians' fascination with the colonial Mexican *elites* (and their written texts) makes them blind to *popular* pneumatology as the foundational epistemology and hermeneutic of the Guadalupe story.[25]

---

[23] The *Nican Mopohua* being that text which Lasso de la Vega, a *criollo* priest, introduced as "an almost forgotten narrative" telling of apparitions *of Mary*.

[24] See Orlando Espín, "Trinitarian Monotheism and the Birth of Popular Catholicism: The Case of Sixteenth-Century Mexico," *Missiology* 20, no. 2 (1992): 177–204.

[25] Sociologist of religion Ma. Socorro Castañeda makes the same point: "How are we LatinoaX scholars of religion replicating the 'religious elites' conversations' which took place in post-conquest Mexico? In other words, to what extent do we reproduce these conversations

Colonial "New Spain" was very much politically, ideologically, and ecclesiastically still dependent on Spain. And
Spain—at least when the published text of the *Nican Mopohua*
first appeared (in 1649, or about a century after the documented existence of the *devotion*)—was trying to secure
its own national (including its colonial empire's) religious
homogeneity. The fear of Lutherans and Calvinists, and of
"crypto-Jews" and "crypto-infidels," was still real; and talk of
the Holy Spirit in all but the most orthodox of devotional and
theological terms was not common or expected and could
indeed provoke an investigation by the Inquisition.[26]

A parallel and particularly important grounding issue is the
reality and vitality of orality and symbol-making.[27] Orality and

---

with our white Euro-centric colleagues (as non-equals) instead of
daring to read the pulse of the faithful and write from that location?"
(Socorro Castañeda, email message to author, Feb. 2, 2022).

[26] The Inquisition in Mexico was well known for investi-
gating, and severely punishing, accusations of (Lutheran, Calvinist,
etc.) "heresies," or of hiddenly practicing Judaism, Islam, any of the
surviving Native religions, or religions of the enslaved Africans. See
John F. Chuchiak, *The Inquisition in New Spain, 1536–1820: A Documentary History* (Baltimore: Johns Hopkins University Press, 2012),
esp. 274–291, on the persecution and punishments against those
accused of being *alumbrados*, which the Inquisition in Mexico defined
as those who espoused heretical and false claims of new revelations, or
regarding interpretations of Christian revelation, especially in reference to the Holy Spirit.

[27] Orality and symbol-making, among the socially or culturally
vulnerable, have been studied by many since the mid-20th century.
I do not want to digress here, so I refer the reader to the following
respected studies (always keeping in mind, of course, the ironic and
important caveat that these studies are all published and, therefore,
cannot be assumed to be the last or definitive word ... because this

symbol-making are inescapable in Mexican and Latin Amer
ican cultures.[28] More specifically, it is here pertinent to recall
that the Nahua culture of central Mexico (still very much alive
after the Spanish conquest) would have transmitted its holiest
and most fundamental beliefs and wisdom through oral means.
Even after the Nahuatl language became alphabetized,[29] orality

---

word remains unwritten, spoken, performed and symbolized). See
James C. Scott, *Weapons of the Weak: Everyday Forms of Peasant
Resistance* (New Haven: Yale University Press, 1986) and Scott,
Domination and the Arts of Resistance: Hidden Transcripts (New
Haven: Yale University Press, 1990). See also Rodolfo Kusch, *Obras
completas*, vols. 1–3 (Buenos Aires: Editorial Fundación Ross, 2000)
[Kusch was one of Latin America's great theorists of culture and
orality]; Alexis Jardines, *El cuerpo y lo otro: Introducción a una teoría
general de la cultura* (Havana: Ed. de Ciencias Sociales, 2004); María
de la Garza, *Política de la memoria* (Barcelona: Anthropos, 2002);
Boaventura de Souza Santos, *Una epistemología del sur* (Buenos Aires:
Siglo XXI, 2009); Bradd Shore, *Culture in Mind: Cognition, Culture,
and the Problem of Meaning* (New York: Oxford University Press,
1996); John Beverley, *Subalternity and Representation: Arguments
in Cultural Theory* (Durham: Duke University Press, 1999); David
Swartz, *Culture and Power: The Sociology of Pierre Bourdieu* (Chicago:
University of Chicago Press, 1997); Peter L. Berger and T. Luckmann,
The Social Construction of Reality (New York: Doubleday, 1966); and
Darcy Ribeiro, *O Processo Civilizatório: Etapas da Evolução Sócio-
Cultural* (Petrópolis: Vozes, 1979). And of course, Michel de Certeau,
L'Absent de l'histoire (Paris: Mame, 1973); de Certeau, *L'Écriture de
l'histoire* (Paris: Gallimard, 1975); and de Certeau, *La Possession de
Loudun* (Paris: Gallimard, 1990).

[28] This is so, whether the cultures descend from Native peoples
and/or from enslaved Africans or are the negotiated hybrid cultures
we refer to as *mestizaje* and *mulataje*.

[29] Nahuatl, "written" by means of pictographs by the central

and symbol-making remained viable and the most frequent means of transmission among the majority of the Nahua.

When discussing a pneumatological interpretation of the devotion to the *Virgen de Guadalupe*, we cannot forget or downplay its very important (though often not explicit) grounding in the notion of tradition, so crucial to any Catholic theology and worldview. More to the point here, we cannot ignore that there has never been *tradition* without *traditioning*—just as there can be no traditioning outside of or unaffected by culture and power asymmetries. In order to better explain my pneumatological proposal, let me briefly

---

Mexico elites prior to the Spanish defeat of Tenochtitlan's imperial hegemony in 1521, became alphabetized (using the Latin alphabet) towards the early seventeenth century. The white *criolloax* increasingly adopted it as a sign of their "New Spain"-born identity in contrast to the Iberian-born elites. The *Huei tlamahuiçoltica* (which includes the *Nican Mopohua*, where the story of the Guadalupe apparitions is told) was written in alphabetized Nahuatl by the *criollo* priest Luis Lasso de la Vega in 1649. It is pertinent to our discussion that most of the Iberians who came to Mexico (and to the rest of the Spanish colonial empire), during the century following the Columbus trips, were themselves villagers and more likely illiterate; hence, orality and symbol-making would have also been viably alive among them as main means of transmission of faith and meaning. Historians of early evangelization in Latin America all too often focus their research and interest on the official, often ordained, missionaries while apparently ignoring the role in evangelization of the *encomenderos*, their families, and their Iberian employees, of the soldiers and sailors, of carpenters, farmers, and other laborers, and of so many other Iberian villagers who came to try their fortune in the newly discovered lands, often escaping landless poverty in their Spanish villages of origin. They too are forebears of the later *criolloax* and *mestizoax* populations.

revisit and make explicit elements pertinent to our present
discussion, often implied and contained in the notions of tradition and traditioning.[30]

The People Who First "Saw" Guadalupe

In the year 1519, a group of Iberians under Hernán Cortés
arrived on the eastern shores of what today is Mexico. With
them Christianity also arrived. By 1521 the fall of imperial
Tenochtitlan had sealed the Spanish conquest of what was
soon to be called "New Spain."[31]

---

[30] I have spent a significant part of my theological work and
publications, over the past three decades, engaging questions of, about,
and resulting from tradition and traditioning. The reader will understand my returning to some of that work here.

[31] Colonial New Spain continued to grow territorially as Iberians
kept conquering and occupying more and more territories to the
north, beyond what been the Mexica-led Nahua empire. The colonial expansion of New Spain came to a halt in the early nineteenth
century with the declaration of New Spain's independence from
Iberian control. New Spain renamed itself by using a slight variation
of the demonym of the people who had founded Tenochtitlan from
"Mexica" to "Mexico." By independence (Miguel de Hidalgo's *Grito
de Dolores* was in 1810, but the war of independence only ended in
1821), New Spain stretched from the Yucatan peninsula in the south
to the Oregon territory in the north, in a geographic fan that went
from the Pacific Ocean to east of the Rocky Mountains. The French
had a bit earlier forced Spain to cede to them the further eastern
reaches of New Spain—what in 1803 was acquired by the US as the
"Louisiana Purchase." The 1848 treaty of Guadalupe Hidalgo ceded
Mexico's northern half to the United States, after the US invasion
and military occupation of those Mexican territories. It is pertinent
to this book to remember that the populations already inhabiting the

The important and more dominant Native Mesoamerican people to confront the Iberian newcomers and their religion were the Nahua. The term "Nahua" refers to the people whose language was (and is) Nahuatl. They inhabited (and still do) areas of south-central Mexico. In some significant ways, the use of the term "Nahua" parallels the use in ancient Mediterranean times of the term "Hellenic"—more cultural and linguistic than genetic, pointing to a number of related societies and peoples in a geographic region.

The Nahua had migrated to the central valley of Mexico after the fall of the Toltec empire, which occurred with the destruction of Tula ca. 1170 CE. During the thirteenth and fourteenth centuries CE, the Chichimec (a broad group of clans), the Alcohua, the Tepanec, and the Mexica all came from the northern region of present-day Mexico and occupied abandoned towns and lands in the central valley or conquered the weakened resident populations. The new arrivals came to be collectively known as the Nahua. Once settled in the Valley of Mexico, these groups proceeded to assimilate Toltec culture and came to believe themselves to be the legitimate heirs of that highly respected civilization.[32]

The Mexica and their city—Tenochtitlan—had become politically, economically, and militarily dominant among the

---

lands that were ceded in 1848 were never consulted regarding their becoming part of the United States. They found themselves conquered again, which led to their being treated as a second-class population by the new occupiers.

[32] The Nahua seem to have viewed the Toltecs much as the ancient Romans viewed the Greeks. The name "Aztec" is derived from *Aztlan*, the name given to the Nahua (and especially Mexica) legendary land of origin "to the north."

Nahua during the early fifteenth century CE. Under Tenochtitlan's lead, a Nahua alliance had been expanding imperially
over non-Nahua peoples prior to the arrival of the Spaniards.

Mostly urban dwellers, the Nahua built stratified societies.[33] Many of these were highly evolved and sophisticated by
any standard. Certainly, the Spaniards were impressed by the
magnificence, the organization, and the technological advances
they encountered among the Nahua. But social stratification
also kept the majority of the population (in Nahua and Nahua-
controlled lands) in clearly ancillary roles.

Furthermore, the high philosophical thought of the elites,
with which the Iberians interrelated and which they preserved
in their colonial chronicles, was clearly not the thought of the
vast majority of the population. This distinction—"popular"
and "elite"—is important when we attempt to understand
the sixteenth-century's Nahua religious beliefs and practices,
because historical sources have tended to limit themselves
(because of their scholarly methodologies and assumptions)
to texts written, or artifacts created, by or for elites before and

---

[33] On the Nahua peoples about the time of the Iberian conquest,
from an immense bibliography, see James Lockhart, *The Nahuas after
the Conquest: A Social and Cultural History of the Indians of Central
Mexico* (Stanford: Stanford University Press, 1996); Bernardo de
Sahagún, *Florentine Codex: General History of the Things of New Spain*
[trans. by Charles E. Dibble and Arthur J.O. Anderson of Sahagún's
sixteenth-century *Historia general de las cosas de la Nueva España*],
13 vols. (Salt Lake City: University of Utah Press, 1950–82); Miguel
León-Portilla, *La filosofía nahuatl. Estudiada en sus fuentes* (Mexico
City: UNAM, 1959); León-Portilla, *The Broken Spears: The Aztec
Account of the Conquest of Mexico* (Boston: Beacon, 1992); and Jacques
Soustelle, *Daily Life of the Aztecs on the Eve of the Spanish Conquest*
(Stanford, CA: Stanford University Press, 1961).

after the Iberian conquest. It is clearly relevant to acknowledge also that the Nahua under Tenochtitlan had become an imperial power—and no people conquer and subdue others without violence, biases, and injustices. Much can be admired among the Nahua, but much cannot.[34]

Few literate peoples have been so profoundly religious as the Nahua. Religion was not just an integral part of their culture. Indeed, there was nothing as important or as "real" for them as the supernatural or religious dimension of existence. They were passionately and sincerely pious, perhaps to an extreme. The Nahua held that since all of existence was held together, and then only barely, by the gods, it was their people's obligation and responsibility to make sure that reality was kept alive by their constant service to the divinities. Indeed, this sense of the precariousness of life seems to have led to a profound sense of existential anguish in Nahua culture, although balanced by much beauty, cultural pride, and (elite) philosophical depth.

As the city of Tenochtitlan became the capital and center of their empire, the Mexica elites produced arguably the most impressive literature of any people in the Americas before the Iberian conquest. Through their "painted" books and other written sources (e.g., inscriptions on walls, monuments, statues, etc.) we get considerable information on Nahua religion. We also have a significant body of literature describing the Nahua, written by Nahua and/or Iberians after the conquest.

Nahua religion had been a modified mirror of the Toltec one, at least until the Mexica reform led by Tlacaelel, who

---

[34] Should it surprise us that the Tlaxcala people, and others subjugated by the Nahuas, allied themselves to Cortés, hoping that a Nahua defeat would bring about their own liberation? History proved their hope naïve. Cortés only brought about a change in masters.

was the "power behind the throne" to several Tenochtitlan kings between 1426 and 1480 CE. This reform changed the self-image the Mexica had had of themselves, made them empire-builders, and convinced them of the incessant need to "feed" the Sun in order to guarantee the continuation of reality and of human existence. Tlacaelel taught his people that they were *the* people of the Sun, and that by divine election their most crucial mission was to keep the Sun alive—because if they failed to do so, reality would collapse into utter chaos. The Mexica mission to "feed" the Sun, and so keep reality going, was the fundamental religious motive and legitimation of Mexica empire-building wars and administrative genius. The capture of victims for human sacrifice (more specifically, for offering living human hearts), needed to "feed" the Sun, became one of the most important and frequent reasons for warfare. Indeed, the so-called "flowery wars" were organized with the sole purpose of capturing sacrificial victims.

Nahua traditional religion seems to have existed in an "elite" version, sanctioned and promoted by the state, and in a "popular" version that was the most likely religion of the majority of the people. The elite version, obviously, is the one we know best because it belonged to the educated and the powerful. Books, temples, and other monuments usually reflected the elites' version. While I am in no way implying that the two forms of Nahua religion were somehow inimical to each other, it is evident that the elites had developed a highly sophisticated theological and philosophical reflection on the meaning of divinity, of life, and of the cosmos that was not easily accessible to the majority. The elite religion had a theological understanding of God and of the gods that did not reflect the working people's belief in the actual existence and daily activities of hundreds of gods. The popular version of the Nahua religion believed in the real, distinct existence of the gods and in more gods than the elite counterpart. What were regarded by the elites as "expressions" of the supreme god were regarded as separate divine beings by most people. The myths of the elite were more frequently thought of as "sacred stories" whose wisdom was immensely more important than the story told, while the myths repeated by the regular folk were usually taken to literally convey what the story told.[35]

Nahua traditional religion (elite and popular)[36] believed in one supreme god, *Ometéotl*—"god of the twos." This supreme deity was one dual god in whom the opposites were integrated—e.g., visible/invisible, masculine/feminine, tangible/intangible. The first and most original (and originating) god, the source of all that exists, *Ometéotl* was the only uncreated god

---

[35] The differences among the elite and popular Nahua seem to have been grounded in access to economic and political power and not on differences based on theologies or doctrines. Degrees of cultural "sophistication" in their respective understandings and uses of myth and symbol seem to have established the real differences between the Nahua elite and popular religious constellations. Access to "sophistication" has much more to do with location in hegemony's power asymmetries and less with conceptual abilities or conclusions. Furthermore, "sophistication" is itself a term that assumes a power-located, non-innocent perspective.

[36] Besides the bibliography on the Nahua, cited in preceding notes, see Laurette Séjourné, *Burning Water: Thought and Religion in Ancient Mexico* (New York: Grove, 1960); David Carrasco, *Religions of Mesoamerica*, 2nd ed. (Long Grove, IL: Waveland, 2013); and Mary Miller and Karl Taube, *An Illustrated Dictionary of the Gods and Symbols of Ancient Mexico and the Maya* (New York: Thames and Hudson, 1997).

and was known by many titles. For example, *Tlóque 'Nahuaque* ("the owner of the near and close") was the most excellent of those names and it signified closeness, intimacy, interiority, as well as omnipresence. *Ollintéotl* ("the divine movement') suggested that the supreme god was the source or origin of all existence. *Ipalnemohuáni* ("the one because of whom we live") indicated that *Ometéotl* was also the source of all meaning— and meaning was the most fundamental quest of Nahua religious thought. *Moyocoyáni* ("the one who created himself") pointed to *Ometéotl* as the uncreated, original god. And *In nelli in téotl* ("the true god") implied that this supreme god was truly and really divine, like no other.

Ometéotl was the source of human thought and freedom. One of the supreme god's contributions to humanity was precisely the ability to doubt, because it led to reflection and wisdom. *Tezcatlipoca* ("smoking mirror") might have been at one point, perhaps before the Toltec past, the most visible expression of *Ometéotl*, but by the time of the Nahua, *Tezcatlipoca* had become fundamentally associated with royal power and with ruling dynasties.

In elite Nahua culture and religion, all the gods were somehow believed to be "manifestations" or "expressions" of *Ometéotl*, or "personifications" of *Ometéotl*'s various attributes. In popular Nahua culture, however, the gods (with few exceptions) were considered to be distinct beings in themselves, although the same god was frequently known by several different names.

In the extraordinarily elaborate mythology of the Nahua, *Ometecuhtli* ("the lord, the one of dual divinity") is the masculine representation of the supreme divinity. In this guise it stands for the divine, creative force, the divine semen that

enters *Omecihuatl*; and its symbols are the stone and lightning.
Omecihuatl ("the lady, the one of dual divinity") is the feminine manifestation of *Ometéotl*, and consort of *Ometecuhtli*,
with whom she forms the creating pair. *Omecihuatl* represents the divine womb that makes development and growth
possible. Her symbols are earth and serpents and a skirt
made of stars. *Coatlícue* ("the one with the skirt of serpents")
is similar to the earth goddess and is really only the first title
or expression of *Omecihuatl* herself. The mother of the gods,
she is both creator and destroyer, a synthesis of life and death.
Tonantzin ("our true mother") was one of the titles or expressions of *Coatlícue*. In other words, there is in the Nahua myths,
elite and popular, a direct connection between *Tonantzin* and
Ometéotl—the former being the expression of *Coatlicue*, who
expresses *Omecituatl*, who in turn is the eternal feminine in
and of *Ometéotl* (the supreme god).[37]

Inherited from the Toltec past are two other important
divinities: *Tlaloc* ("the juice of the earth") who was god of
rain and main guardian of all agriculture and of peasants, and
Quetzalcóatl ("feathered serpent"). *Quetzalcóatl* was the god
of self-sacrifice and abundance. Responsible for the existence
of present reality ("the fifth Sun"), *Quetzalcóatl* created it by
going to the underworld and stealing the bones of ancestors
from earlier realities (i.e., from the preceding "Suns") and then
making himself bleed on them. *Quetzalcóatl* discovered corn

---

[37] The Mexica reforms promoted by Tlacaelel also completed the
exclusive identification of their particular clan's main god (*Huitzilopochtli*, "blue hummingbird of the left") with the Sun, and many
earlier myths related to Sun and Moon were then transferred to
and applied to *Huitzilopochtli*. The Sun must be "fed" by his people
through offerings of living, beating human hearts.

and gave it to humans. He kept the sky from collapsing onto earth and united the heavenly with the earthly, matter with spirit. A later myth said that he fled Tula and reached the Gulf of Mexico coast. There he built a boat in order to reach Tlíllan Tlapállan ("the place of wisdom"). Another myth, abused by Iberian conquerors in the sixteenth century, promised *Quetzal-cóatl*'s return from the sea.

Teotihuacan ("where the gods are made") was the most sacred city in Mesoamerican history. It was first settled around 400 BCE. Several groups arrived later from the Gulf of Mexico coast, bringing with them the traditions and rituals that in time would become the cults of *Tlaloc* and *Quetzalcóatl*. The city had been important as a cultural and religious center even before the Toltec and much before the Nahua. Teotihuacan was built around broad processional boulevards and the two monumental pyramids dedicated to the Sun and to the Moon in honor of the deities who had sacrificed themselves there. Not surprisingly, Tenochtitlan—the Mexica capital—was rebuilt to parallel the grandeur and sanctity of ancient Teotihuacan. Tenochtitlan's majestic processional boulevards, which crossed at the large ceremonial center where the main temples were, impressed all visitors including the conquering Iberians, who praised the Mexica capital for its beauty, magnificence, and size. All Nahua cities seem to have been built with their important ceremonial role in mind.

Worship rites were presided over by priests who were usually celibate and of unkempt appearance. These men had attended school and were specifically trained for a life dedicated to ritual and prayer. Besides the solemn and very public rites involving human sacrifice (i.e., the offering of beating human hearts), all Nahua participated in many other religious ceremonies dictated by the exact calculations of their calendar and by the daily estimates of their priests. There were daily rituals and weekly ones; some were held during the daytime hours and others at night; every month witnessed city-wide ceremonies; and every number of months and of years there were further rites. Every fifty-two years, the Nahua feared that the Sun would collapse, so the most solemn and anguished religious services were held on that occasion, to make sure that the Sun would continue shining and the world would not end. The Nahua (and specifically the Mexica) liturgies were highly elaborate, regardless of the occasion.

Nahua traditional religion also believed in an afterlife, a sort of earthly paradise in the Sun. Warriors fallen in battle and women who died in childbirth received the highest reward from the gods and were immediately taken to paradise. Daily life was not considered as desirable as an honorable death.[38]

In Forced Dialogue with the Iberians

The Iberian Catholicism that was brought to the Americas, beginning with the Columbus voyages, was Christocentric, and it seems not to have emphasized the Holy Spirit. Naturally, the Trinitarian doctrines on the Holy Spirit were taught and Trinitarian expressions were included in liturgy, piety, and art, but they resembled in no way the emphasis placed on Christ.

---

[38] A thorough study of the Nahua traditional religion of ancient Mexico requires far more detail and complex analyses. Our purpose here, however, is to give the reader a sufficient set of interpretive tools to understand the point and reason of our pneumatological proposal. The cited bibliography can lead the interested reader to further study of the Nahua religion.

The Spirit was constantly named and invoked, but in manners befitting the religious ambience of sixteenth-century Spain.

It must be recalled that Iberian Christianity (especially in Extremadura and Andalucía, from which Cortés and most early colonizers had come) had just emerged victorious, at the end of the fifteenth century, over more than seven hundred years of Muslim rule and cultural domination. The so-called *Reconquista* had been slow and bloody—a contradictory process of learning to live with and from the enemy while fighting the enemy.

The experience of the *Reconquista* also affected religious understanding and pastoral practice, as can be expected. Basic doctrinal agreement had been needed in order to guarantee some fundamental cohesiveness to an Iberian peninsula divided into competing Christian kingdoms.[39] Also given past European experiences with popular appeals to the authority or role of the Holy Spirit, Spain's Christians were often not inclined to dwell on the "third person" of the Trinity in their theological reflections and pastoral practices. Unity in religion

---

[39] The reader must understand that during the entire medieval period, doctrinal and liturgical standards among Iberian Christians were set regionally and sometimes even locally, within the very broad context of the shared ancient conciliar creeds and Patristic-era liturgical practices. Political unification, however, which was bringing increasingly together the disparate Iberian Christian kingdoms, required some doctrinal and liturgical uniformity. Uniform standardization across worldwide western Catholicism was an outcome only of the post-Tridentine period. Very relevant here is church historian (and historian of doctrines and theologies) Gary Macy's chapter "The Iberian Heritage of US Latino/a Theology," in *Futuring Our Past: Explorations in the Theology of Tradition*, ed. Orlando Espín and Gary Macy (Maryknoll, NY: Orbis, 2006), 43–82.

was needed in relation to Islam, and it somehow seemed to Spain's Christians that to emphasize the action of the Holy Spirit (beyond that which was needed for orthodoxy) was to invite a potentially dangerous divisiveness. In the sacral world of late medieval Iberia, and within the context of the *Reconquista* process, this outlook probably seemed reasonable. When the *alumbrados* finally appeared on the Spanish scene, with their emphasis on the Holy Spirit, they had to face the power of the Inquisition. The few sixteenth-century *alumbrados* in the Americas were even more swiftly dealt with.[40]

In other words, in late medieval Spain, any discourse on the Holy Spirit, beyond that which was necessary to guarantee doctrinal orthodoxy, was interpreted to be a potential source of religious and civil disunity and a possible source of heresy; as a consequence, this discourse was to be avoided in order not to jeopardize unity among Christians and their common effort against the Muslim "infidels."

The same can be said of the Spanish attitude toward preaching about the Holy Spirit in Mexico, except that the "infidels" in Mexico were not Muslim.

Christianity arrived in the Nahua world with Cortés and the many who followed him after 1519. But it arrived stained by the blood of conquest, as legitimizer of the violence and atrocities the conquest involved, and as sustainer and justification of the cultural invasion of the Nahua that soon followed

---

[40] See Melquiades Andrés Martín, *Historia de la teología española en el siglo XVI*, 2:227–259, 601–603; Bernardino Llorca et al., *Historia de la Iglesia Católica* (Madrid: Biblioteca de Autores Cristianos, 1967), 3:601–640; León Lopetegui and Félix Zubillaga, *Historia de la Iglesia en la América española* (Madrid: Biblioteca de Autores Cristianos, 1973), 1:438–445.

their military defeat. Christianity did not arrive innocent. It
crossed the Atlantic uninvited, carried by imperial hubris and
might. The Nahua could not avoid dealing with Christians
who regarded themselves as unmistakably superior to the
Nahua and their beliefs. Iberian ethnocentrism, greed, and
violence—much more than Iberian theologies—placed the
Nahua under the heel of Christians. And it was there, under
the heel of Christian conquerors, that the conquered were
supposed to hear the Gospel.[41]

It is also true that among the Christians there also came a
few others, still beneficiaries of the conquest and of imperial
might, who nevertheless attempted to share their Christian religion with the Nahua "infidels" within less inhumane contexts
and through less inhumane means.[42] But how many missionaries
were there in the growing waves of Iberian arrivals in New Spain?

---

[41] Throughout Latin America, the parallel realities of violence
and vanquishment were the context for evangelization. See Luis
Rivera Pagán, *Entre el oro y la fe. El dilema de América* (Río Piedras:
Universidad de Puerto Rico, 1995); Rivera Pagán, *A Violent Evange-
lism: The Political and Religious Conquest of the Americas* [trans. of
Rivera Pagán's masterful *Evangelización y violencia. La conquista de
América*, 1991] (Louisville: Westminster/John Knox, 1992); and, of
course, Gustavo Gutiérrez, *Dios o el oro en las Indias* (Lima: Centro de
Estudios y Publicaciones, 1989).

[42] There were, in Mexico and in other areas of Latin America,
some courageous missionaries who defended the Native populations
(e.g., Las Casas, Montesinos, Valdivieso). Yet the majority of missionaries probably did little, or thought they could do nothing, to stop
the genocidal behavior of most Iberian colonizers. Many missionaries,
one must admit, could be also counted among the willing abusers and
predators of the Natives, their lands, and their cultures.

Much more numerous were the lay Iberians who had left their villages and their poverty on the other side of the Atlantic and were now willing participants in the violent takeover of the "New World." They too shared their Christian religion with the Nahua population, although the Natives with whom these Iberians interacted were often the ones in the lower echelons of Nahua society. While the recognized missionaries often entered into dialogues and other exchanges with the Native elites—and these encounters are frequently reflected in the colonial chronicles they wrote—they did not seem to have clearly understood that all of the conquered did not share the same perspectives or experiences as the (also conquered) Native elites from whom the missionaries often sought explanations.[43] As we saw earlier, the Nahua religion, like every religion known to humankind, conceived and displayed internal diversity (in its holy stories, practices, rituals, and ethics) due to the varied social and cultural locations of the members of the religions

---

[43] See Louise Burkhart, "Pious Performances: Christian Pageantry and Native Identity in Early Colonial Mexico," in *Native Traditions in the Postconquest World*, ed. Elizabeth H. Boone and Tom Cummins (Washington, DC: Dumbarton Oaks Research Library and Collection, 1998), 361–381; Burkhart, *The Slippery Earth: Nahua-Christian Moral Dialogue in Sixteenth-Century Mexico* (Tucson: University of Arizona Press, 1989); Burkhart, "'Here Is Another Marvel': Marían Miracle Narratives in a Nahuatl Manuscript," in *Spiritual Encounters: Interactions Between Christianity and Native Religions in Colonial America*, ed. Nicolas Griffiths and Fernando Cervantes (Birmingham, England: University of Birmingham Press, 1999), 91–115; and Burkhart, *Holy Wednesday: A Nahua Drama from Early Colonial Mexico* (Philadelphia: University of Pennsylvania Press, 1996).

in their societies' grids of power asymmetries. The Nahua and
the Christian religions both reflected their internal diversity in
sixteenth-century Mexico, and thereafter.

But who evangelized the Nahua? Evidently, Iberian Christians. Which is to say, historically, the ones who did not and
could not represent (or present) uniformly identical religious
beliefs, explanations, rituals, and practices because of their
varied social and cultural locations in both Iberian and colonial
societies' power asymmetries. Furthermore, the religion Christians presented and represented, historically, both defended
and abused the Natives and continued to legitimize the depredation of their lands and cultures—for the sake of greed, or for
the sake of God.

What could the Nahua have understood regarding what
they were told was "Christianity"? Whom could they understand? Given the pneumatological interest of the present
volume, I will mainly focus on Trinitarian and specifically
pneumatological evangelization in the early colonial Nahua
context and thereafter.

Trinitarian evangelization outside of European cultural
contexts is difficult. This is due to several historical and cultural
elements.

First of all, the doctrines concerning the Trinity have been
expressed, ever since the councils of Christian antiquity, through
the cultural and linguistic vehicles of Mediterranean, European
philosophical traditions. Prior to the nineteenth century, no
sustained serious attempt was made by mainstream Christian
theologies to escape this cultural and linguistic straightjacket,
the efforts of the Jesuits Matteo Ricci in China and Roberto
de Nobili in India perhaps being exceptions.[44] And since in

---

[44] See Joseph Dehergne, *Répertoire des Jésuites de Chine de 1552*

western Europe—before, during, or after the various Reformations—these doctrines had not raised the passionate arguments among Christians that would have led to a development of thought and language beyond early conciliar creedal categories, Trinitarian evangelization in and from western Europe was (and often has been) held hostage to Eurocentric linguistic and cultural thought patterns.

Some popularized catechetical explanations of Trinitarian doctrines have in fact often confused the very contents they tried to simplify, leading to either practical crypto-tritheism or undistinguishing, strict monotheism among most western Christians. Church preaching on the Trinity has repeated either classic creedal language or popularized simplifications. Trinitarian language (which at the same time must refer to the core of Christian belief in one God) seems still impermeable to the changed and changing languages and notions of Christians, remaining fixed in its early Eurocentric statements. One example of Eurocentric domination in Trinitarian language is the continued use of the term "person," despite the fact that this word today bears little or no resemblance to the meaning(s) of the Latin *persona* during the Patristic period, employed in the West as a translation of the Patristic Greek *prosopon*. This language faces the same issues today. Trinitarian expressions, among Christians, cannot be reduced to ortholalic repetition[45] of creedal statements.

à 1800 (Rome: Institutum Historicum Societatis Iesu, 1973) and Peter Bachmann, *Roberto Nobili: 1577–1656* (Rome: Institutum Historicum Societatis Iesu, 1972).

[45] See Orlando Espín, "Ortholalia," in *Introductory Dictionary of Theology and Religious Studies*, ed. Orlando Espín and J. Nickoloff (Collegeville, MN: Liturgical Press, 2007), 993.

A second element that often hinders Trinitarian monotheist evangelization outside of European contexts seems to
be the fact that most culturally non-European human groups
have found no reason to have the thought patterns and
worldviews necessary to understand Trinitarian monotheism
until they (these human groups) became "objects of interest"
for the Eurocentric. This, of course, raises other important
questions about cultural invasion in the name of religion, and
about the possibilities of (and obstacles to) interculturation[46]
of the faith.

A third element, mostly a consequence of the first two,
has to do with the means historically chosen to communicate
Trinitarian doctrine. There is no question that catechetical,
evangelization channels can and do determine what, to what
degree, and in what way the hearers of the proclamation
understand and accept it. The cultures of the evangelizers
and of the hearers, and their prior theological understandings or possibility of understanding a given component of the
Christian message should lead to this or that choice of communication vehicle. Nevertheless, when cultural differences or
violent hostilities between missionary and hearer are deep,
the possibility of successfully finding intercultural means of
evangelization seems unlikely, while a proclamation resulting
in ortholalia appears more likely. And if that which is incom-
pletely presented (because of the absence of intercultural means
or because of the presence of dehumanizing, violent contexts)
is the very core of Christian Trinitarian monotheism, then
the foundations of newly planted Christianity are dangerously

---

[46] See the section on "Interculturality" in ch. 1 as well as the
section "Interculturated in 'New Worlds'" below.

weakened. Unless the hearers demonstrate otherwise—to the surprise of the evangelizers.

It would be impossible to document all the cases and arguments pertinent to this discussion. We are here discussing sixteenth-century Mexico and how Trinitarian monotheism (in particular, pneumatology as expression and part of Trinitarian monotheism) was taught to the Nahua populations. In pointing out what seem to have been the inadequacies of Trinitarian monotheist evangelization in sixteenth-century Mexico, I am explicitly suggesting that the conquest's contexts that made possible Christian proclamation also made possible its cultural reinterpretation or reformulation by the evangelized in manners ortholalic and also orthodox, unforeseen and unexpected by the (lay and ordained) missionaries.[47]

The Nahua were told[48] that there was only one God, who

---

[47] I have been struck by the frequency with which Christocentric evangelization appears to flourish where Trinitarian proclamation does not seem to be as successful. Without creating false or unacceptable doctrinal separations between christology and Trinitarian theology, it might be interesting to follow this intuition through research and to discover whether the latter confirms the former, since it seems theologically obvious that the christological and the pneumatological can have no foundation other than the Trinitarian.

[48] We know this because we have many of the catechisms and chronicles from the period. See, for example, Sahagún, *Historia general de las cosas de la Nueva España* and Toribio de Benavente (Motolinía), *Historia de los indios de la Nueva España* [critical ed. of Motolinía's 1541 original, with notes and introduction by E. O'Gorman] (Mexico City: Ed. Porrúa, 1979). Early sixteenth-century Mexico produced Native masterpieces that today are misleadingly called the "Testerian manuscripts" because they were at first wrongly assumed to have all been created by Jacobo de Testera, a Franciscan missionary in

is three, who are one. What could they have understood?
And how could and did they express what *they* understood?
Would the Nahua notion of a supreme, originating divinity as
the inclusion of parallels and even of opposites give them the
cultural tools to engage and come to an understanding of what
Christians meant by Trinity?

In seeking these answers we have to keep very much in
mind that most Nahua learned about Christianity through lay,

---

sixteenth-century Mexico. These catechisms and prayer books—very
different from other visual devices used during the same period—were
formed by pictographs that represented the doctrinal and ethical
teachings that the Iberian missionaries attempted to communicate to
the recently conquered Native populations. The authors of these catechisms were very frequently themselves members of the vanquished
communities who were acting as interpreters between their people
and the missionaries. In these manuscripts the Native authors and
artists employed some traditional, pre-conquest pictographs as well as
totally new ones to convey the doctrines of victorious Christianity.
Though there seems to have been some type of control by the friars
over the Native authors, the fact that many of these manuscripts have
glossed explanations (written by the friars) that do not follow the
pictorial explanations (drawn by the Native authors) tends to indicate
that the missionaries could not impose Christian concepts without
significant cultural filtering done by and through the Native authors.
Since official doctrinal communication depended very frequently
on these pictorial catechisms, and these in turn were culturally and
freely drawn by Natives who had recently entered into contact with
Christianity, the message received by the larger Native populations
evangelized through these pictographs could have been "more" than
the teaching of the friars. See Narciso Sentenach, "Catecismos de la
doctrina cristiana en jeroglíficos para la enseñanza de los indios ameri-
canos," *Revista de Archivos, Bibliotecas y Museos* 4, no. 10 (1900):
599–609 and Espín, "Trinitarian Monotheism and the Birth of
Popular Catholicism."

Iberian villagers—who had a self-serving and far from innocent access to the Nahua world as a consequence of violent
conquest. On the other hand, the more "sophisticated" Nahua
engagement with Christian Trinitarian doctrines was limited
to their religious elites' conversations (again, as non-equals)
with the Christians' own missionary elites. And elites are elites.

Importantly, the one element of Iberian Catholic Christianity that pervaded both villagers and missionaries (and
every other popular or elite segment of the Iberian dominant population) in New Spain was Marian devotion. Marian
images became very common and very much present in religious buildings, large and small, as well as in Iberian homes
and public spaces in New Spain. Distribution of paintings
and images of Mary, as well as involvement in Marian proces-
sions, prayers, etc., soon became widespread among the Nahua
too. Benefitting from James C. Scott's study and insights
on "hidden transcripts" among those conquered or socially
dominated,[49] we can seriously wonder to what degree Marian
symbols and devotional practices did not become means to
other ends among the Nahua. Precisely to the point, anthro-
pologist Louise M. Burkhart underlines that

> when the Spanish invaders suppressed the Nahua's
> public religion and offered the cult of the saints in
> exchange, Mary became the most important sacred
> female available for Indigenous adaptation. Coming
> from a tradition in which female divinities were
> significant players and the sacred was conceived in
> male-female duality or complementarity, the Nahua

---

[49] See Scott, *Domination and the Arts of Resistance*.

were predisposed to grant importance to the only
major female figure presented to them by Christianity
… Marian devotion dovetailed Nahua concepts and
practices in more than simply as a replacement for
outlawed goddess cults.[50]

I would further Burkhart's statement by suggesting, for the
same reasons, that expressing the Ultimate Mystery as "relationship" was clearly within the Nahua cultural universe, as it
was and remains among Christians.

It is evident that Iberian Christians gendered (masculin-
ized) their understanding of the relationship ("Trinity") they
believed was the Ultimate Mystery because of their histories
and cultures but not because God's being requires masculin-
ization. The Nahua, also because of their culture and history,
understood the relationship that is the Ultimate Mystery in
binary, complementary terms that led to gendered binarization
of the Supreme Being: believing that the one *Ometéotl* is two,
who are one.

Consequently, if the terms "Father," "Son," and "Holy
Spirit" are human expressions that attempt to truthfully
"say" the One beyond all expressions in the Christian
understanding,[51] so are the terms *Ometecuhtli* and *Omecihuatl* in the Nahua understanding of the Ultimate Mystery.
Identical in content? No, clearly. And neither group of terms,
Christian or Nahua, is either less or more human, insufficient,
culturally crafted, and historically bound. If we were ever to

---

[50] Louise M. Burkhart, *Before Guadalupe: The Virgin Mary in
Early Colonial Nahuatl Literature* (Albany: Institute for Mesoamerican Studies/SUNY, 2001), 4–5.

[51] As we have already discussed in earlier sections of this book.

think, as Christians, that we can actually understand or intellectually capture the Trinitarian being of God because of and through our sincere repetition, sophisticated explanations, and use of the traditional doctrinal terms, we would again and again need to be reminded by Augustine of Hippo: *Si comprehendis, non est Deus*.[52]

God *is but is not* what we say or affirm.[53]

It is thus not difficult to reasonably affirm that many of the Nahua,[54] upon hearing of the Christian God as relational trinity (a message frequently accompanied in public by Marian devotions), could have easily transferred the *devotional symbols* associated with Mary (the only Christian female sacred figure) to the "Holy Spirit," given the culturally understandable roles the Spirit played within the Trinitarian relationship as commonly understood in sixteenth-century Iberian Catholicism.[55] "Mary

[52] See also Espín, *Idol and Grace*, 77–84, 98–112.

[53] Apophatic theology is a welcome and much needed interlocutor in intercultural understanding and, especially, in intercultural theologizing.

[54] Given what Burkhart underlines in her work, what other specialists have demonstrated that further confirms Burkhart's work as well as what we have been discussing throughout the pages of this book.

[55] See Yves Congar, *I Believe in the Holy Spirit*, 3 vols (New York: Seabury, 1983) and Andrés Martín, *La teología española en el siglo XVI*, 1:296–309, 356–426 and 2:107–297. Indispensable are Pablo Richard, ed., *Materiales para una historia de la teología en América Latina* (San José, Costa Rica: Departamento Ecuménico de Investigaciones [DEI] and Comisión de Estudios de Historiade la Iglesia en Latino América [CEHIL] 1980); Richard, ed., *Raíces de la teología latinoamericana*, (San José, Costa Rica: DEI/CEHIL, 1985); and Evangelista Vilanova, *Historia de la teología cristiana* (Barcelona, Spain: Herder Editorial, 1989), 2:693–731. See also, earlier in this chapter, the bibliographic references to the sixteenth-century *crónica*s

became the most important sacred female available for Indigenous adaptation," writes Burkhart.[56] Therefore, I underline again
that I am *not* suggesting that Mary became divinized. What I
am suggesting is that the Holy Spirit came to be expressed in
manners possible in a new cultural context—manners unforeseen or misunderstood by the Iberian conquerors and their
missionaries.[57] The Nahua's symbolic ortholalia in time led to
symbolic orthodoxy among them, if I may be allowed the categories—i.e., an effective tool originally intended for survival
became, in time, a true pneumatological expression. Iberian-
imposed orthodoxy, in the sixteenth and seventeenth centuries'
context of conquest and of forced Christianization, could not
but lead to reinterpretations among the vanquished.

Religious art had been, throughout Europe, the more frequent
means to tradition the Christian doctrines regarding the Trinity
and, therefore also, doctrines regarding the Holy Spirit.[58] It soon

---

by Motolinía and Sahagún, as well as the *catecismos* ("Testerian" or
not) created in early colonial Mexico.

[56] See Burkhart, *Before Guadalupe*; the entire volume merits
careful study and consideration.

[57] A new context, forced upon Native populations by Iberian
Christian conquest and violence. These forced the Nahua to survive
by trying to understand what the newcomers demanded that the
Nahua accept. However, what was understood could only be publicly
expressed (by the Natives) through the symbols and categories acceptable to the conquerors. The Nahua now had to express and share in
Iberian Christian modes.

[58] I find very important, on "traditioning" the "Tradition"
through public religious art, the work done by my University of San
Diego colleague Susie P. Babka. We have had, over the years, many a
conversation on this topic. See her book, *Through the Dark Field: The
Incarnation through an Aesthetics of Vulnerability* (Collegeville, MN:

also became the more common missionary means and visual aid to teach about the Trinity in early post-conquest Mexico.[59] But little concerning the Holy Spirit has survived from this period. We are reduced to noticing the typical dove-like representations that appear in some surviving colonial paintings and those that have been carved in a few churches' and convents' *retablos*, most notably two carvings in the church of San Bernardino in Xochimilco.[60]

Rare and tangential references to the Trinity included the dove figure, but nowhere have I found any depiction, in sixteenth-century colonial art, that moved beyond this one representation, and no particular theological or pastoral significance seems to have been attached to it.

The second half of the colonial period as well as the decades after independence from Spain, but not the early sixteenth century, saw a consistent increase in awareness of and devotion to the Holy Spirit. It is clear that the later *cofradías* of the Holy Spirit would have been unthinkable in the doctrinal climate of the earlier colonial period.

There are obvious references to the Spirit in the frequent use of the *per signum crucis*[61] and in the Trinitarian invocations

---

Michael Glazier, 2016).

[59] See Eleanor Wake, *Framing the Sacred: The Indian Churches of Early Colonial Mexico* (Norman, OK: University of Oklahoma Press, 2010), esp. 171–234; Noé Esquivel Estrada, ed., *Arte en el siglo XVI. Arquitectura y pintura en el estado de México e Hidalgo, y teatro franciscano en México* (Toluca, Mexico: Editorial Torres/UAEM, 2010); Abelardo Cabrillo Gariel, *Autógrafos de pintores coloniales* (Mexico City: UNAM, 1953), 147–165; and Francisco A. Schroeder, "Retablos mexicanos," *Artes de México* 106 (1968): 11–28.

[60] See Schroeder, "Retablos mexicanos."

[61] *"Por la señal de la santa cruz …"* And the even more frequent

and doxologies in the celebrations of baptism, Eucharist, and the other sacraments.[62] Many of the established prayers to be said in private also included Trinitarian formulae. The people, therefore, were supposedly reminded of the Spirit through liturgy and other prayers. But what did they understand? Our sources do not allow us to say more than what we have already stated. And, given the importance of the subject, that is precious little indeed. What stands out as a visual constant throughout early colonial Mexico, and thereafter, is the dove as the (almost) exclusive representation of the Holy Spirit,[63] and Marian symbols as the only feminine sacred representations allowed by the victors.

Interculturated in "New Worlds"

In the early sixteenth century, a "new world" began in what today is southern central Mexico. A "New World," claimed the Iberians and other Europeans; but in 1519 it was "new" only to them and not to that world's many inhabitants, who had

---

"*En el nombre del Padre y del Hijo y del Espíritu Santo*" with which all popular and most liturgical prayers began and ended.

[62] It is important and relevant to recall that until the pertinent decrees of the Second Vatican Council (1962–65), the official Catholic liturgy was celebrated in Latin, a language not understood by the majority of lay Catholics across the world. We can easily suspect that Latin was a further barrier for the Nahua in the sixteenth and seventeenth centuries and thereafter.

[63] In the visual art that attempted to depict the Trinity, the constant imagery included an old man, a younger man, and a dove between them, all three surrounded by expressions of grandeur or power (even when the younger man might be portrayed carrying a cross, which for the Nahua would not have been a known object with religious significance, much less an object implying torture and death).

called it their home for many centuries. Nevertheless, because of the violent post-1492 arrival and subsequent violent conquests by the Iberians and other Europeans, a new world began too for the Native populations of Mexico and of the entire western hemisphere, as well as for all newcomers and their descendants. Throughout and after five centuries, new worlds have continued to be constructed by the beneficiaries of conquests, by their heirs (the *criolloax*), and the heirs of the Native peoples, of the enslaved Africans forcibly brought to the "new" lands to create wealth for Christians who thought God had given them the right to enslave other humans, and of the growing majority of *mestizoax* and *mulatoax* throughout the hemisphere.

It is not surprising that the victors imposed their Christian religion. What is surprising is that it was interculturated[64]— and not by the conquerors, but by the conquered![65]

---

[64] "Interculturated," yes. I remind the reader that the understanding of "interculturation" I use here is *not* coextensive or synonymous with the more common meaning of the term "inculturation" in present-day Christian theologies. I refer the reader to the section on "Interculturality" in the first chapter of this book for a more thorough explanation of what I mean by the term, and for the reasons why I distance myself from the common and still colonizing use of "inculturation" in many of today's Christian theologies. I again underline the importance (indeed, indispensability) for any discussion on inculturation and/or interculturality of the work by internationally renowned philosopher Raúl Fornet-Betancourt and, of course, of the "hermeneutic architecture" created by Antonio Gramsci's notions and processes of "hegemony" and "historic bloc." Bibliographies and comments on Fornet-Betancourt and Gramsci have been included in this and the preceding chapters' notes.

[65] Of course, there are exceptions to the statements I have just

Among the intercultural realities were the experiences
and beliefs associated, in Catholic Christianity, with the Holy
Spirit. This led to unforeseen expressions—unforeseen by both
conquered and conqueror.

We cannot forget that interculturation is not equal to
dialogue. Dialogue assumes that the participants are equals.
But interculturation is not a dialogue of equals. Specifically, it
is not a process between or among equal cultures.

As this process occurs in history (and certainly as it occurred
in sixteenth-century Mexico, and in the rest of what we call
Latin America) it is a process engaged by some cultures in order
to survive foreign cultural invasion. Interculturation is a matter
of survival. The cultural invaders have access to the culture of the
invaded not by the latter's choice and strength but by the latter's
vanquished status. The invaders, because of their success at
conquest, have the power to force their categories and languages
(and not just the spoken ones) on the conquered, at least in
public. If the conquered learn to employ the cultural categories

---

made, and necessary nuances to be made. But, by and large, Christianity
was *adopted and adapted* by the Natives, the Africans, the *criolloax*, and
the various "intercultural" descendants of all of them. I should again
emphasize that *mestizaje* and *mulataje* were and are, first and foremost
but not only, part of the cultural processes of interculturation, including
where undeniable racial intermingling processes have been and continue
to be. And so—as two examples among many—it is possible to affirm
that a "white" Mexican—if culturally identifiable as Mexican—is
thereby culturally *meztizoax*; and that a "white" Cuban—if culturally
identifiable as Cuban—is thereby culturally *mulatoax*. Internalized
racism might make some uncomfortable with such identifications
(*mestizoax, mulatoax*), but culturally there is no doubt that such identities are as real and as cultural as "Mexican" and "Cuban" are.

and expressions (linguistic or not) of the conqueror, the latter will claim success and their "obvious superiority."

For the conquered, however, another reason led to the employment of the cultural categories and expressions of the victors: survival, above all. Although the categories or expressions came with the conqueror, their public use was molded by the conquered. And their public use soon fashioned an interpretation that allowed the vanquished to survive as themselves while somehow engaging the victor as victor.

In other words, the Nahua knew and recognized that the Iberians had won. The new issues for the Nahua were about survival *as Nahuas* while inevitably dealing with the conquering Iberians. The Nahua could not pretend that the fall of Tenochtitlan and of their "world" had not occurred. In a world imbued in and molded by sacral cosmovisions[66] and assumptions, their engagement with the victorious Christian "sacred" became a matter for survival. Interculturation became important and, arguably, inevitable.

The Nahua had to accept Christianity, or at least appear to have accepted. Interestingly, in their cosmovision, the unexpected and swift victory of the Christians also meant that the latter's "God" had defeated the Nahua's own. It was for the Nahua's safety and interest to attempt to understand and appease the new, conquering God.[67] This God was said to be

---

[66] Both Nahua and Iberian. It is arguably more comprehensive (and probably more accurate) to speak of "cosmovisions" rather than "worldviews." See Raúl Fornet-Betancourt, Nicole Note, Josef Estermann, and Diederik Aerts, eds., *Worldviews and Cultures: Philosophical Reflections from an Intercultural Perspective* (New York: Springer, 2010), esp. 69–87, 181–190.

[67] Robert Ricard does not exaggerate when he claims that he found

one who is three who are one, and who is/are always accompanied by a "sacred woman" who is not one of these three who are the one.[68]

The sixteenth century was evidently and understandably a period of deep crisis for the Nahua. It could not have been otherwise. The people's identity had been shaped by their conviction that they were the "People of the Sun," charged with the extraordinary responsibility of feeding and keeping the Sun alive. Now that identity was deeply challenged and its grounding responsibility made impossible. The world had collapsed at the onslaught of a new, unknown "God."

But the Nahua heard that the new God had created all that exists and had been willing to die for the good of humankind, while also empowering, guiding, and comforting humans, so they could do the will of that new God. That the Supreme God was the source of all that exists was not something the Nahua doubted, just as they did not doubt the Supreme God's omnipotence, omniscience, and presence to and within all.[69]

---

in the early colonial missionaries' *crónicas* multiple references to large numbers of Nahua and of other central Mexico's Indigenous peoples approaching missionaries and asking for instruction in Christianity. His interpretation regarding the Natives' reasons, however, is very much blind to the Natives' need to survive and to their cultures. See Robert Ricard, *The Spiritual Conquest of Mexico: An Essay on the Apostolate and the Evangelizing Methods of the Mendicant Orders in New Spain, 1523–1572* (Berkeley: University of California Press, 1982).

[68] Again, see Burkhart, *Before Guadalupe*.

[69] They believed that the Supreme God, who was uncreated ("he created himself"), was more present to/within us than we are to ourselves. *Tloque 'Nahuaque* was the title of the Supreme Originating God, who is both and equally "near and far." See León-Portilla, *La filosofía nahuatl.*

That the conquering God of Christians had suffered and died *also* for the benefit of vanquished Nahua was surprising—especially when reality was becoming increasingly painful to them. But a God who suffers for others, without immediate victory, was not unheard of in the Nahua world.[70] It is interesting that, despite depictions of the Trinity's grandeur in early colonial art, the "Son" is most frequently depicted crowned with thorns, on a cross or by a cross, dying and bleeding, and by himself, except for the accompanying presence of "the only sacred female" permitted to the Nahua by the Iberians.[71]

To do the will of the victorious God was important. Survival depended on it. The Nahua were told that God was also empowering, guiding, and comforting humans, so they could do the will of that God. They soon learned from the missionaries and other Iberians that the Christian God was always spoken of in exclusively masculine terms and referred to through exclusively masculine nouns, although the Nahua were also told that God had no gender. The Christian God was one who was three who were one—but who was the

---

[70] The notion of *atl-tlachinolli*, widespread in the Nahua world, allowed the Nahua to think of and refer to a single concept or a single god by employing pairs and opposites. The very name of the notion ("water-fire") was used to refer to war—a single term for a complex meaning that incorporates the opposites. See Miller and Taube, *Gods and Symbols*, 41.

[71] The phrase is from Burkhart, *Before Guadalupe*, 4–5. See also Jennifer Scheper Hughes, *Biography of a Mexican Crucifix: Lived Religion and Local Faith from the Conquest to the Present* (Oxford: Oxford University Press, 2010) and Orlando Espín, "The God of the Vanquished: Foundations for a Latino Spirituality," *Listening: Journal of Religion and Culture* 27, no. 1 (1992): 70–83.

third? Attempting to understand Christians because survival depended on it, the Nahua saw the frequently displayed dove who, besides its artistic depictions and inclusion in Trinitarian formulas to begin or end prayers ("*En el nombre del Padre y del Hijo y del Espíritu Santo*") seemed absent from daily speech, explanations, or devotions.[72] Who, then, was called on to lead the Nahua to the Christian God, and to discover and do (indispensably for their survival) God's will? Who had *de facto* become the symbol and bearer of empowering, of guidance, and of divine *apapacho*?[73] The only authorized female sacred figure!

Could the Nahua have understood, with orthodox doctrinal nuances and in the early sixteenth century, the Christian beliefs of "incarnation," "virginal conception," "divine maternity," and others? Did most of the Christians who had arrived in Mexico understand these beliefs with their orthodox doctrinal nuances?

---

[72] I remind the reader of the difficulties of pneumatological talk, and of references to the Holy Spirit, in the Iberian world immediately preceding and immediately following the fall of Granada in 1492, as well as after the 1517 start of the European reformations and counter-reformations. It is also important to remember that, also in Iberia, *visual* references to the Holy Spirit had come to be almost, though not totally, reduced to the dove.

[73] *Apapacho* (and the verb *apapachar*), in Mexican usage since colonial days, means something like cuddle, caress, "embrace with the heart," tender touch. The term is an adaptation into Spanish of the Nahuatl *papachoa* or *papatzoa*, which means to "soften with the hands." Grandmothers, mothers, spouses, and friends are very often the culturally expected givers of *apapacho*, which is an affective, sensed sign of solidarity, support, and trust. Grandmothers and mothers are especially expected to *apapachar* their grandchildren and children, regardless of the latter's age.

The Nahua saw and heard, and soon joined in, the words said and hymns sung to the only sacred female who accompanied Iberian Christianity. They heard of her and saw the Iberians' devotion to her. They were told she was the "mother of the Son." It was she that the Iberians beseeched for empowerment, for guidance, for *apapacho*, and for understanding God's will. The Christians trusted that she would do for them as an *apapachante* and guiding, empowering (grand)mother would and should.

Did the Nahua identify the only authorized sacred female with Mary of Nazareth? To do this they would have needed prior cultural—including doctrinal—categories or tools to do so. My argument is that, *through their need to survive*, they tried to understand the Christian God. They also saw the Iberians engage (besides, despite, beyond, and even with, all the doctrinal catechetical explanations and nuances) in an *apapachante*, empowering, and guiding *relationship* with the one sacred female figure that Christians called "Mary." Given the Nahua cosmovision and their own religious inclination to regard the Supreme Divine mainly in relational (including feminine) terms, and their living through the difficult sixteenth-century historical moment, it would be surprising if the Nahua had *not* used the symbols, expressions, and rites, associated with the Christian Mary to understand, symbolize, express, and ritualize the even more Christian "Holy Spirit"—now visualized not as a dove but as the sacred female.[74] Not Mary but the Holy Spirit: the one who guides, *apapacha*, and empowers.

---

[74] I remind the reader again that the power asymmetries in sixteenth-century Mexico, and the real violence that came with the Iberian conquest, determined and limited the symbolic alternatives available to the Nahua for expressing what they understood of Christianity.

The "new worlds" of sixteenth and post sixteenth centuries Mexico engaged in a process of interculturation that permitted the vanquished to find meaning and survival by their own reinterpretation of the Christian Divine, acceptable in content but expressed (and thus reinterpreted) to include the feminine and, more explicitly, the maternal. Perhaps implied (but not authorized as public expression) was the unexpectedly orthodox "*en el nombre del Padre y del Hijo y de la Madre*."[75]

The ancient Christian adoption of the symbolic expressions *ruach*, *parakletos*, *pneuma*, dove, and fire, to speak of the Holy Spirit, are no more necessary or transparent than *madre*—and just as limited and cultural. Among most of those who are not allowed power and who are victimized by power asymmetries, *madre* is clearly much more empowering, guiding and *apapachante* than other symbols, and therefore, more transparently pneumatological.[76]

---

[75] I am in no way suggesting that mothers are always representative of the best in humanity. Mothers can be humanizing, supportive, and welcoming, but they too can abuse and dehumanize. When we use "Father" or paternal language for God, we are all too aware of the many limitations the term can express among humans. When we use "Mother" and "maternal," we should be just as aware. And yet culturally, among very many Mexicans, Mexican Americans and Latinoax in general, there is in families a special emphasis on mothers and their affective maternal roles, even while mothers can fall short of these cultural expectations. The exact same awareness should be present when we speak of the "masculine" and of the "feminine."

[76] Again, unless we choose to fall into idolatry, we have no alternative but to concede that Christian symbols and expressions for the divine are not *necessary* to the divine, do not "contain" the divine, and are certainly not absolute or irreformable.

The symbols incorporated onto the painting of Guadalupe were acceptably Marian, but I suspect the *relationship* with her (during and after the sixteenth century) has been much more complex and telling. Why the early connection between Guadalupe and Mary? To answer we need to ask further: *Who* was doing the connecting?

So … Pentecost at Tepeyac?

On the hill of Tepeyacac,[77] outside of Tenochtitlan, on the sacred site the Nahua had dedicated to "our Mother,"[78] the conquerors from Iberia's Extremadura region had built a chapel dedicated to the Marian devotion associated with their region of Iberia—the Virgin of Guadalupe.[79] A silver statue of their

---

[77] "Nose-like mountain," in Nahuatl. We have become used to the subsequent shortening of the original term to Tepeyac.

[78] Recall my earlier statement: "There is in the Nahua myths, elite and popular, a direct connection between *Tonantzin* and *Ometéotl*—the former being the expression of the maternal of and in *Coatlicue*, who expresses *Omecituatl*, who in turn is the eternal feminine in and of *Ometéotl* (the supreme god)."

[79] The Extremaduran *Virgen de Guadalupe* was popular among the early colonizers because it had been very popular, throughout several centuries, among Christians engaged in the Iberian *Reconquista* movement. This Guadalupe was a popular Marian symbol of the movement. For this and for what follows, see also I. Rubio and G. Acemel, *El real monasterio de Nuestra Señora de Guadalupe* (Cáccrcs, Spain: HH. de Heraclio Fournier, 1951) and Bernal Díaz del Castillo, *Historia verdadera de la conquista de la Nueva España* (Mexico City: Porrúa, 2009). See more details and references in Poole, *Our Lady of Guadalupe*. Hernán Cortés and the earlier Iberian colonizers were mostly from Extremadura.

Extremaduran Guadalupe was placed in the *retablo* over the main altar. But soon thereafter, the painting we today associate with Guadalupe was placed on a side wall in the chapel.[80] When the Nahua started visiting the chapel, they ritually danced and brought offerings to the female figure on the painting—to the dismay of some of the early missionaries who saw "worship" and not "devotion," which would have implied (in the minds of the missionaries and of other Iberians) a "pagan" and not a Christian expression.[81] The missionaries

---

[80] On the origin and history of the painting there are, as expected, several theories. The *Nican Mopohua*, of course, explains it as a miraculous event that followed several apparitions of Mary. However, most scholars have (over more than a century) suggested that a Nahua artist of the early sixteenth century—known by the Spanish name Marcos Aquino—was the creator of the painting of Guadalupe. In his 1556 sermons, Franciscan friar and superior Francisco Bustamante explicitly refers to a Native artist named Marcos as the painter.

[81] As time passed, Franciscans and other missionaries adopted, adapted and promoted the devotion to "Mary" of Guadalupe, but their first responses to the Guadalupe of Tepeyac were clearly very negative. Bustamante (the Franciscan superior) and Sahagún (the noted Franciscan missionary and *cronista*) vehemently denounced the "idolatrous worship" they saw towards Guadalupe of Tepeyac. See Yongho Francis Lee, "Our Lady of Guadalupe in Bernardino de Sahagún's *Historia general de la cosas de la Nueva España*," in *New Frontiers in Guadalupan Studies*, ed. Virgilio Elizondo and Timothy Matovina (Eugene, OR: Pickwick, 2014), 1–18, esp. 9–18; Josef Kroger and Patrizia Granziera, *Aztec Goddesses and Christian Madonnas: Images of the Divine Feminine in Mexico* (Burlington, VT: Ashgate, 2012), 228–236; Poole, *Our Lady of Guadalupe*; and Richard Nebel, *Santa María Tonantzin, Virgen de Guadalupe: Continuidad y transformación religiosa en México* (Mexico City: Fondo de Cultura Económica, 1995).

bemoaned and attempted to put an end to the dancing and the offerings, but they did not succeed. Not long thereafter, the painting hanging on the side wall was transferred to the *retablo* over the main altar, and the Extremaduran statue of Guadalupe was melted into silver candelabra placed on either side of the painting. Decades later, the narrative in the *Nican Mopohua* began to circulate, but by then the Guadalupe of Tepeyac had become increasingly popular in Tenochtitlan and environs. Miracles attributed to her fueled her popularity, as in any religious context they would, especially when most of the beneficiaries of her miracles were said to be the vanquished.[82]

Why the early connection between Guadalupe of Tepeyac and Mary? And *who* was doing the connecting given that, by the missionary *cronistas'* own admission, the Marian connection was not evident among the Nahua who came to "worship" at Tepeyac?

We have a sense of the difficulties, including violence, that accompanied and molded the lives of the Indigenous popula tions in sixteenth-century south-central Mexico. The fear of the Inquisition was real. The fear of being accused of crypto-paganism was real. The continued depredation and abuses by the victorious Iberians were real. To survive, many among the Nahua leadership became collaborators of the European conquerors.

In the 1500s there was little hope that any new devotional, religious practice born among the Nahua, especially one claiming to be Christian, could survive in Mexico without

---

[82] Very relevant here is the demonstrable fact that the devotion *preceded* the claims of apparitions. In fact, the devotion's development seems to follow a colonial typology *for nearly a century before* some *criollo* priests claimed to "recall" the narrative of apparitions.

raising questions or leading to investigations or repression. We already saw that the presence of the new painting of Guadalupe on Tepeyac was received with strong opposition and mistrust by the missionaries. And yet this Guadalupe survived and came to replace the Extremaduran one.

Throughout sixteenth-century Mexico, all Marian devotions were imports from Iberia. But by the dawn of the seventeenth century, there grew among the emerging *criolloax* elites an inclination to emphasize what was "typical" of "Mexico." The revival of the Nahuatl language (using the Latin alphabet) among the *criolloax* is evidence of this, as well as their inclination to underline the uniqueness of "Mexico" vis-à-vis Iberia.[83] The *criollo* clergy, and many among Hispanicized Nahua, apparently Marianized Guadalupe as part of *their* movement to underline that "God has chosen Mexico," and that Mary had "appeared" in Mexico.

The *Nican Mopohua* is one example of this *criolloax* drive to underline the uniqueness of Mexico. The text was published in 1649 by the *criollo* priest Luis Lasso de la Vega.[84] At the time he was the chaplain at the Guadalupe chapel on Tepeyac, where he had succeeded Miguel Sánchez, another *criollo* priest,[85] who was apparently the first (in 1648) to

---

[83] These emphases on the "uniquely Mexican" would, in time, crystalize into a national identity that then led to the struggle for independence. Not surprisingly, Guadalupe became the religious banner of the early nineteenth-century independence movement.

[84] The long complete title, published in alphabetized Nahuatl, was *Huei tlamahuiçoltica omonexiti in ilhuicac tlatocaçihuapilli Santa María totlaçonantzin Guadalupe in nican huei altepenahuac Mexico itocayocan Tepeyacac*. One of its chapters was the *Nican Mopohua*.

[85] See Miguel Sánchez, "Imagen de la Virgen María, Madre de

mention a Marian apparition. Lasso de la Vega attributed the authorship of the *Nican Mopohua* to a Nahua nobleman named Antonio Valeriano, who had been a student of the *cronista* and missionary Bernardino de Sahagún in the Franciscan school for young men of the Nahua nobility—the same Sahagún who had vehemently fought against Natives' dancing and offerings when the Guadalupe painting was first placed in the chapel on Tepeyac.[86] Valeriano eventually became rector of this school, and later the Spanish colonial authorities appointed him governor of a significant portion of the Nahua region surrounding Mexico City. If Valeriano was the author of the famous text of the Guadalupe apparitions, he would have very surely known of the opposition Sahagún, Bustamante, and other Franciscans displayed against Guadalupe; and he would have also known that the only way to tell the story was to Marianize it, given that no other sacred female figure was authorized. It is also an issue that there are no documentary references to the story told by the *Nican Mopohua* for the century prior to Sánchez and Lasso de la Vega.[87] If the original version of the *Nican*

Dios Guadalupe, Milagrosamente aparecida en la Ciudad de México. Celebrada en su historia, con la profecía de los doce del Apocalipsis" [original of 1648], in *Testimonios históricos guadalupanos*, ed. Ernesto de la Torre Villar and Ramiro Navarro de Anda (Mexico City: Fondo de Cultura Económica, 2005), 153–267.

[86] Is it farfetched or unreasonable to suppose that Valeriano (if in fact he was the author of the *Nican Mopohua*) might have been "convinced" by his missionary teachers that the only possible "orthodox" interpretation of that painting was a Marian interpretation?

[87] Lack of written texts does not equate to lack of reality. But, if what the *Nican Mopohua* presents as known and as fact were well

Mopohua was written during the sixteenth century, there is no surviving copy and no surviving evidence of *any* version earlier than the one published in 1649.

The majority of the Nahua under colonial rule, however, were not like Antonio Valeriano, who collaborated with the victorious Iberians and became governor over his own people by the authority of the conqueror. Nor were the Nahua like the *criolloax* and their search for a "Mexican" identity. Guadalupe of Tepeyac came from the Nahua and they remained her greater devotees. *Whom* did *they* find in and through her?

And is it still the same after five centuries? Mexican and Mexican American cultures today can no longer be simply (or romantically) understood as descendants of the Nahua and the Iberians, because there were, and still are, many other Native cultures in Mexico, and because five centuries of events and history do not pass without impact and transformation. What might have been the sixteenth-century Nahua understanding of "who" is venerated on the Tepeyac, is not the same as today's Mexican and Mexican American understandings—because,

---

known throughout sixteenth-century Mexico City, it is hard to explain the complete absence of any documentary mention of the apparitions of Guadalupe prior to 1648. A century of silence? There is religious art and there are documents that attest to a *devotion* to Guadalupe of Tepeyac prior to 1648 (See Bernal Díaz del Castillo, *Historia verdadera de la conquista de la Nueva España* [n.p.: FV éditions, 2020]; Sahagún, *Historia general de las cosas de la Nueva España*; and Poole, *Our Lady of Guadalupe*), but this is in no way the same as claiming that there was knowledge or memory of any *apparition*. Nevertheless, I must acknowledge that oral traditions do exist, survive, and often confound the assumptions of contemporary western historians and theologians. "Could," however, is not coextensive or synonymous with "did."

demonstrably, most twenty-first-century Mexicans and Mexican Americans are not familiar (or not as familiar) with the cultures and religions that violently met after 1521. Most Mexicans and Mexican Americans today would identify as Catholic[88] and not as practitioners or followers of the ancient Nahua religion. Who is it, then, that present-day Mexicans and Mexican Americans find in and through Guadalupe?

The reader has by now divined that my answer to the question is "the Holy Spirit." Furthermore, in Guadalupe the people have expressed—in a culturally authentic way—the Catholic Christian belief that God empowers, *apapacha*, and guides. Because Marian symbols and expressions were (and are) authorized, they have been borrowed and transferred to say what generations of Mexicans (and not just the colonial-era Nahua) understood and understand of God—because what *Mexicans* understood and understand of the Christian God is evidently and also "maternal" (besides being creator "Father" and suffering "Son").

In this book's first chapter, I brought to the reader's consideration that what we say in and through one cultural, symbolic, linguistic, and socioeconomic context might not mean or allow for the same meaning in a different cultural, symbolic, linguistic, and socioeconomic context. No context can pretend that its particular expression and meaning exhausts or expresses all that could be expressed or meant. In fact, to convey the same meaning might require, by unavoidable cultural and historical re-contextualizing, seemingly different (or even

---

[88] Even if non-practicing, many Mexicans and Mexican Americans would still claim to be Catholic or at least to be devotees of Guadalupe.

apparently opposing) means of expression which will, in turn, probably unveil new or different depths or dimensions of and in the meaning.[89] This, I think, is what occurred in reference to Guadalupe, and continues to occur.

Centuries of *criolloax* dominance, of Catholic androcentrism, and of marginalization of the non-Eurocentric have continued to veil the pneumatological underlayers of Marianized language. Nevertheless, devotion is, first and foremost, *not practices but relationship*, and when the relationship is pneumatological in quality, texture, and expectations—which is as most people *relate* to the *Virgen de Guadalupe*—it is with the Holy Spirit they relate, regardless of what the veiling language of the Eurocentric might hope to conceal or convince.[90]

Even today, vulnerable Latinoax in the US are not free from the consequences and realities of hegemonic dominance and continued adverse attempts at controlling and manipulating their experience, their families, and their religion. Latinoax are not "authorized" to publicly state and express themselves and their faith in *their* culturally authentic ways and expect respect. The beneficiaries of dominance (often the learned and often the ordained) still appear to think that they can express better, and understand better, than Latinoax can understand or

---

[89] As we have discussed regarding the western reasons for adding *Filioque* to the creed of Nicaea, in order to prevent an Arian interpretation of the conciliar text after its translation into Latin.

[90] I find indispensable, regarding Mary as pneumatological symbol of God, theologian Leonardo Boff's reflections. A direct and well-argued summary of his contributions appears in the chapter "The Holy Spirit, Giver of Life, and the Feminine Element" in his recent book, *Thoughts and Dreams of an Old Theologian* (Maryknoll, NY: Orbis, 2022).

express themselves about themselves, a hegemonic attitude not much different from the one that dominated the "new world" that followed the sixteenth century on the western shores of the Atlantic.

If we pay attention to the quality and texture, the dynamics, the hopes and expectations of the *relationship* devotees have with Guadalupe today, it is clear that these are not describing a relationship with Mary of Nazareth. The dynamics, hopes, expectations, and quality of the devotee-Guadalupe relationship, expressed by and in it, "define" the "mother" in terms not Marian but divine. Guadalupe hears and acts, she heals and guides, empowers and comforts, *apapacha*, and even demands—without regarding herself as an intercessor. The devotees do not regard her as merely interceding. She is the mother who acts, of her own volition and out of her own love for her children. And this, because she is not merely a human.

But if not merely a human who merely intercedes, then Guadalupe is not and cannot be merely a symbol expressing Mary, the human mother of Jesus. In other words . . .

Let us recall now all we have discussed regarding the possibilities and limitations of all pneumatological expressions. Let us remember what Christians have attempted to say about the Spirit of God, and which experiences of the empowering and *apapachante* God led them to use their respective cultural terms to express their experiences and faith. Let us also recall that women in the Latinoax extended family (especially mothers and grandmothers) are indispensable pneumatological hermeneuts of Guadalupe.

If one were to seek out and identify the more crucial Latinoax daily relationships, the importance of women would immediately shine. They are leaders and interpreters of the extended family's religion, values, and morals. But most importantly, women are the ones with whom Latinoax sustain the most meaningful and deepest daily relationships. These women have been responsible for the survival and resilience of Latinoax daily cultures and lives.

Latina women gave us life and nourish it among us by their affection, protection, and hard work, either as heads of single-parent family units, as necessary breadwinners, and/or as homemakers. They teach and counsel us, empower the best in us and forgive our failures, touch our hearts and minds with questions and wisdom, and open hopes and dreams for our lives. They are our refuge in childhood, our co-conspirators in young love, our guides toward responsible adulthood, our steadfast rock in suffering, and the positive validation of our talents and lives. Latina women (mothers, grandmothers, aunts) are also our families' wise interpreters of religion and of the heart of God, the teachers of ethics and the leaders of our prayers. They are our extended families' living sacraments of God and the sacred. These women are, above all else, the ones with whom all Latinoax usually relate in the deepest and most meaningful of ways.

In pneumatology we have customarily used the Hebrew and Hellenic *ruach*, *pneuma*, and *parakletos*, aware that these terms point ultimately to the empowering Spirit of God. In the Latinoax cultural *cotidiano*, the pneumatological seems to be *madre* or *abuela*—because she is the guide, the empowerer, the advocate, truthful and trusted critic, sustainer and advisor, interpreter of "God's heart," welcoming and comforting embracer.[91]

---

[91] I refer the reader again to Titizano's remarkable "Mama Pacha: Creator and Sustainer Spirit of God."

That is why the maternal (and consequently the Marian) can be expressions of the Spirit of God. *Madre* teaches us to be wise by understanding and learning from our *experiencia de vida*, leading us to have courage because God is always with us. She displays, bears, and translates, in our cultural contexts, the gifts of the Spirit of God.

If we remember, acknowledge, reflect, and pay careful attention to Latinoax familial realities, we can affirm that the *Virgen de Guadalupe*[92] is a culturally authentic symbol expressing God's Holy Spirit, even if today there are many who are still not allowed (or are afraid) to use *Madre* to name the One who is one with the "Father" and the "Son." A pneumatology from the people allows us—in fact, dares us!—to subvert the androcentric and Eurocentric assumptions we too often encounter in Christian speech, piety, and doctrinification.

In Conclusion:
Pneumatologies from the People

We need pneumatologies that deal not only or mainly with doctrines, doctrinal claims, and/or symbols for the Spirit of God—doctrines, claims, and symbols that do not historically dismiss the *ongoing relationship* of humans with the Spirit (and of the Spirit with humans) in the theological and existential understandings. What we have learned regarding the relationship of very many Catholics with the *Virgen de Guadalupe* suggests that we must consider that relationship's subversion of established claims and explanations, most of which ground

---

[92] And again, not Mary, the mother of Jesus. But is Guadalupe the only case?

themselves in androcentric, Eurocentric, and aporophobic[93] cultural assumptions.

These cultural assumptions have shaped "official" and "learned" doctrines, pious symbols, and liturgies. But as we discussed earlier, all talk, thought, or symbol of the Ineffable Divine Mystery is inescapably no more than a human construct, necessarily bound by and to the sociocultural and transient realities of humans and of all human constructs. The Ineffable Mystery is beyond all and bound to none; but all *we* say, know, understand, and experience regarding God is inescapably human and thus creaturely. To deny this is idolatry.

Pneumatologies Cannot Downplay the Message of the Reign

Pneumatologies from, and traditioned by, the real people who are the real Church,[94] raise subversive alternatives to

---

[93] Aporophobia, derived from a Spanish neologism, refers to rejection, fear, and/or hatred of the poor. See also below my expression "disdain of the destitute."

[94] I remind the reader that the Church is not the ordained but the baptized. This is the doctrine, despite too often being downplayed in practice or forgotten by the ordained and the learned. It is evident that the vast majority of the baptized in the history of Christianity, as well as today, have been the poor, who too often lack real access to education, healthcare, housing, and equality. The immense majority of Christians, since the birth of Christianity, have been the vulnerable and oppressed. They are as capable of faith and the commitments arising from faith as are the ordained and the learned. To claim otherwise is to deny the Christian gospel. It is also extremely important that we recall that Jesus of Nazareth was a landless peasant from a small village in an unimportant part of the Roman empire, and that he spoke

the assumed pneumatologies. To see and understand this, it is very important (in the reflections that follow) to keep in mind that, in most Catholic cultures, women, not the ordained or the learned, are demonstrably the real people's first traditioners.

What we say and experience about the Holy Spirit cannot ignore the subversive message preached by Jesus of Nazareth. The news about the dawning Reign of God is absolutely central to Jesus's living and preaching and to his getting killed by the powerful and rejected by those in religious leadership who collaborated with the occupiers. The news of the dawning Reign of God is also central to understanding Jesus's resurrection. Jesus announced that God had begun to transform *this* world into a radically new world *here*, where God and God's love reign. Jesus further announced that God is calling us to participate in the transformation of this world by asking for our commitment to lives of solidarity, especially with the most destitute and vulnerable. This world is being transformed, and we are called to commit here to this transformation, first and foremost by lives of compassionate solidarity. To believe this message and to publicly commit to and live by its demands is what makes a human "Christian." Nothing else.[95]

---

mainly to those who were like him. He was crucified for committing the "crime" of standing for solidarity with the most disposable of his day and land, discounting the arguments of those religious leaders who collaborated with the occupiers. To claim that Jesus is risen is not about his power but about the truth of his message. God would not raise a liar. Espín, *Idol and Grace*, and also José Comblin, *The Holy Spirit and Liberation* (Maryknoll, NY: Orbis, 1989).

[95] See Espín, *Idol and Grace*, 1–8, and the bibliography cited there, especially William R. Herzog, *Prophet and Teacher: An*

If the news of the dawning Reigning of God is the core of Jesus' preaching and living, it would then be inexplicable that we talk about the Spirit of God in ways that seem more focused on our piety, on our well-being, and on an "out of this world" salvation. The Galilean Jewish peasants with whom Jesus lived and spoke (because he was one of them) did not know of immortal human "souls," and humans "going to heaven" would have sounded blasphemous. For Jesus, and for his Galilean peasant contemporaries who believed him, there could not be salvation without subversion—the radical subversion of this world into one fully according to the compassionate will of God. And to demonstrate that Jesus spoke the truth, God raised him from the dead. God would not raise a liar.

Consequently, pneumatologies have to be subversive too—because pneumatologies cannot ignore or consider secondary for pneumatology the subversive message that Jesus preached, for which he died, and for which God raised him. Furthermore, pneumatologies have to be subversive because they must try to understand and explain the Holy Spirit (to the degree that humans can) as discerner, sustainer, challenger *for the subversion of this world*. The subversion of this world has begun and the new world's reality is dawning. The Spirit "in-spires" humans to discover that Jesus was raised, because he spoke the truth. But agreeing with what Jesus said is a meaningless act unless the agreement leads (without excuses) to *living and acting as builders of the Reign of God here*: this is what it means to be a disciple.

Introduction to the Historical Jesus (Louisville: Westminster/John Knox, 2005); Richard Horsley, *Jesus, Justice and the Reign of God* (Louisville: Westminster/John Knox, 2000); and Horsley, *Jesus and Empire: The Kingdom of God and the New World Order* (Minneapolis: Fortress, 2002).

Did the conquered Nahua and the Mexican generations that followed until today experience the Mexican Guadalupe in these pneumatological ways? I do not think it difficult to affirm that, yes, throughout the centuries, as well as today, her devotees have not hesitated to relate with Guadalupe in pneumatological ways. Why have they not named her explicitly divine? For the same reasons that the *criollo* priests had to "recall" apparitions of "Mary"—Eurocentric, androcentric, and aporophobic Iberian biases could not accept or tolerate any representation or expression of the Christian God except in Eurocentric and androcentric expressions. To claim that the conquered could find their own expressions would be just as unacceptable—unveiling the "disdain of the destitute" in Eurocentric, androcentric pneumatologies.

To accept the expressions of the poor, and their ways of relating with the Spirit of God, as only "quaint" and/or solely "pious" demonstrations of their "insufficient" understanding or of their inability to grasp theological and doctrinal nuances, is deeply problematic. This is so because the theologies, doctrines, and cultural assumptions thereby implied, and often repeated by the dominant, bear the stench of bigotries and self-idolatries historically typical among the Eurocentric and racially white. The message of the "Reign of God" that Jesus of Nazareth announced was not conveyed through the categories or expressions of the dominant or "sophisticated," but by the story-telling, life examples, and gestures that the poor would understand as "God is transforming this world, to include us as equals."

The *Virgen de Guadalupe* is a clear expression and implicit interpretation of the Holy Spirit of the Gospel, opting for the poor and disdained as inescapable indication of God's commitment to the transformation of this world into a new one where solidarity is the foundation of equality. Guadalupe is seen and experienced as "on the side of" the vulnerable—a transparent indication of God's solidarity. The divine "preferential option for the poor" is coextensive with God's demand that there be a radical subversion of this world—a world built for the dominant who "make" the poverty that makes the poor. God has chosen the poor, says the Gospel, and therefore God's will and God's "Reign" cannot be interpreted to sidestep or disregard the poor by permitting poverty to continue to exist and deeply wound the vulnerable. A world without poverty, bigotries, or inequalities would be a radically different world. It would be a world where "God reigns."

Guadalupe subverted and still subverts the established power relations. She is depicted as a Native woman, looking like one of the conquered. Even the *Nican Mopohua* depicts her as appearing to and speaking with a conquered human in the language of the conquered, and furthermore, correcting the leader of the Church in colonial Mexico.[96] She is related with in terms and by means clearly pneumatological. So the Marianizing attempts have not succeeded in changing the nature of the relationship between Guadalupe and the people.

Guadalupe and Popular Catholicism

With this understanding of Guadalupe as an example, what do pneumatologies from the people look like? These pneumatologies must reflect "the faith of the People." Pneumatologies from the people must subvert the power asymmetries reflected

---

[96] The reader should nevertheless remember my observations regarding the *Nican Mopohua*.

in our sociocultural, ecclesiastical, and doctrinal assumptions, and "the faith of the People" is the paramount launching pad for this process of subversion.

It has been my repeated contention that "popular Catholicism" (i.e., where we find "the faith of the People") is a privileged vehicle for Latinoax cultures.[97] Popular religion has been, and still is, the least "invaded" cultural creation of our people and a locus for our most authentic self-disclosure. It is through popular Catholicism that we have been able develop, preserve, and communicate deeply held religious beliefs and other cultural values. And while popular Catholicism is not the only means for the development and preservation of our cultures, it would be extremely difficult, if not impossible, to think about or understand Latinoax cultures without finding the crucial role that popular religion has played (and still plays) in our midst as matrix and vehicle of many of our most authentic values and selves.

Popular Catholicism (among Latinoax, African Americans, Filipino Americans, and Native Americans, and among the marginalized Catholics all across the globe) is a dynamic complex of symbols, rites, experiences, and beliefs that peoples, feeling themselves marginalized from the so-called mainstream[98] of society and Church, have developed and sustained

---

[97] See Espín, *The Faith of the People* and Espín, *Idol and Grace*. See also Orlando Espín, *Grace and Humanness: Theological Reflections Because of Culture* (Maryknoll, NY: Orbis, 2007); Espín, "Culture, Daily Life and Popular Religion, and Their Impact on Christian Tradition," in *Futuring Our Past*; and Espín, "An Exploration into the Theology of Grace and Sin."

[98] Perhaps, more accurately, "self-designated mainstream" by the dominant in Church and society.

in order to communicate with God, to understand and "image" God, and to experience salvation. Consequently, popular Catholicism is where a culturally authentic subversion starts.

Popular religion is a privileged place of self-disclosure and culture. Through it people experience the life of society and Church from the margins. Through it they say that they are capable of creating and sustaining alternatives. The marginalized have not simply yielded to hopelessness, but rather continue to believe and search for a way to confront their marginalized status. What is presented to them as normative by society and Church is not fully so.

Marginalized Catholics across the world have created their parallel ways to God, to life, and to salvation. They have created, through popular Catholicism, understandings and images of the Divine. Most, however, do not consciously think of their popular religion in these terms.

The means by which popular Catholicism grasps and conveys these motifs are "popular"—but by this I do not merely want to say that they are very widespread, although they certainly are. But these means are "popular" mainly because they literally come from the "people" themselves.[99] It is often hard to discover the historical specifics of when a given symbol began to be used, or a specific rite began to be practiced, or a belief began to be held. Popular Catholicism today, everywhere, is the result of the mostly anonymous contributions of many generations. These contributions are expressed through the symbols, rites, and beliefs that were and are culturally possible or available to people, always somewhat modified

---

[99] "Popular" is the adjective corresponding to the noun "people."

in order to convey whatever experiences, understandings, or motifs needed to be communicated at the time.

Where, and when, the symbols, rites, and beliefs of the "official" Church and dominant society are perceived by the people as unsatisfactory or inadequate (culturally speaking), the marginalized will create their own or improve on those already available.

Though popular Catholicism contains and expresses a great deal of goodness, of faith, and of trust, it also has within it the wounds of the very marginalization against which it wants to rebel. This cultural creation conveys the reality of the people *as it is*. The courage and the fear, the hope and the fatalism, the faith in God and the temptation to magical manipulation, the strength of our families and the *machismo* of patriarchal society, the deep respect for motherhood and maternal courage as well as the stereotyping of women—all these and much more are to be found in popular Catholicism.[100]

To admit these strengths and these wounds of popular Catholicism is to acknowledge that popular religion is a real reflection of reality and of culture. And reality, by and large, is difficult. The social marginalization of the majority of the world's Catholic population, together with their accomplishments, faith, courage and hope, sins, and idols, are all present in popular Catholicism. They create popular religion that in turn shows Catholic people who they are.

---

[100] It is undeniable that the self-appointed Catholic "mainstream" of the dominant also suffers from the many wounds inflicted by the dominant's imperial self-manipulation, and by their assuming their marginalization of others and subsequent power asymmetries as "normal" and "divinely established."

Popular Catholicism is indeed a privileged vehicle of the people's self-disclosure—and of God's.

Pneumatologies from the People

To find out how the vulnerable[101] understand God (i.e., the Divine) is not as easy as it might seem. As peoples who have been marginalized by dominant society—and following Antonio Gramsci on this[102]—Latinoax (the majority of whom in the US are of Mexican descent) have culturally introjected many of the images and ideas about God purveyed by those who are dominant in Church and society. Indeed, part of the dynamics of marginalization is that the marginalized are bombarded with, and partially convinced by, the arguments and reasons of the dominant.

Therefore, if we were to ask Latinoax about God, we would hear much of what we could hear from others in Church and society. Obviously, because most Latinoax are Catholic, at least culturally, their repetition of these ideas and images is due to

---

[101] Again, the vast majority of the real people who are baptized—and who consequently are and have always been the real Church—are vulnerable, marginalized, disregarded, and denied rights and suffer other indignities. It is imperative that we again underline that *theirs* is "the faith of the Church."

[102] I refer especially Gramsci's insights into the dynamics of the "historical bloc" and the "doubts" that remain active among the "subaltern"—despite the apparent success of the "hegemonic" arguments employed by the dominant. Besides the bibliographic references to Gramsci's works in this book's introduction and preceding chapter, see Hugues Portelli, *Gramsci y el bloque histórico* (Mexico City: Siglo XXI Ed., 1980). Portelli's study is among the very best on Gramsci's thought.

their Catholicism. But although this seems to be true, it is also certainly true that Latinoax are Latinoax, and therefore their introjection and expression of doctrines and images about the Divine is still a culturally Latinoax process.

In other words, the very Catholic identity of Latinoax does not cancel or diminish their cultural lenses and identity, but rather must make Latinoax Catholics be Catholic *latinamente*. As I noted earlier, there is no a-cultural Christianity; there never has been. Thus if Latinoax are Catholic (and the majority of us are) then we must be so *latinamente*, or we are not Catholic. And thus, if we are to experience, understand, and image God as Catholics, Latinoax must do so *latinamente*. There is no alternative.

Traditionally, and as we have seen, the experience of the triune God led to the Christian understanding of God as Trinity. Inseparably one, the three "ways" can be distinctly experienced. The Holy Spirit has traditionally been experienced as the One who leads to, empowering and sustaining, a compassionate solidarity that effectively transforms this world into one that is radically according to God's will.

Nothing speaks more clearly about the Spirit of God's presence and work than sustained, concrete, and effective actions that lead to a new reality of inclusion, equality, justice, and solidarity. Ask the victims of society's power asymmetries and they will confirm this. Ask the marginalized by dominant hegemony and they will confirm this. Ask those made vulnerable in society by bigotries based on gender, race, sexual orientation, and ethnic identities, and they too will confirm this. Because nothing speaks more clearly about the solidarious, compassionate Christian God than acts of inclusion, equality, justice, and solidarity.

As a consequence, when the marginalized "speak" (in the broadest sense) of their experience of God in their lives, *there* a pneumatology is born from the people. It might not follow the styles expected in learned theological constructs, because the birthing of real, "truth-full" pneumatologies relies not on theories or bibliographies but on the lived, liberating experiences of the Spirit among the real people who are the real Church.

Acknowledgments

As some readers know, I retired in 2019 after three decades in the department of Theology and Religious Studies (THRS) at the University of San Diego (USD) in California. This intentionally brief volume might be my last, although I smiled while writing the beginning of this sentence.

Because of the significant changes brought by retirement to my life and career, I beg the reader to allow me to gratefully recognize colleagues, students, and friends who have generously engaged me over the many years of my professional life at USD and earlier at other institutions.

This book's dedicatory page expresses my gratitude to many who have been indispensable conversation partners. But there are other important conversation partners whom I must also acknowledge.

I want to thank my USD colleagues, in the THRS department and others, for their support and many insightful conversations over the years. I am very grateful for my USD colleagues' scholarly advice, insightful questions, great conversations—and culinary artistry. Special thanks to Mary C. Doak, Bahar Davary, Russell Fuller, Víctor Carmona, Peter A. Mena, Karen Teel, Susie Babka, Evelyn Kirkley, Emily Reimer-Barry, Lark Díaz, K. Lekshe Tsomo, Christopher Carter, Lance Nelson, Alberto L. Pulido, Gail Pérez, Michelle Camacho, Evelyn Cruz, Jesse Mills, Thomas E. Reifer, and Gary Macy.

I could not have journeyed through this long adventure as theologian and teacher without those who taught and guided me before or during my doctoral studies at the Pontifical Catholic University of Rio de Janeiro (PUC/RJ), and in the years since then.

Conversation partners are indispensable in theology, and over the decades there have been many in California, Florida, the Dominican Republic, Brazil, and Mexico. Many years ago, in classes and conversations, Professors Peter J. Albano, James McGowan, John Freund, James V. Morris, Alfonso García Rubio, Pedro Ribeiro de Oliveira, João B. Libânio, Álvaro Barreiro, Juan L. Segundo, Leonardo Boff, Juan C. Scannone, and Segundo Galilea raised challenging questions that in time led me to embark on this theological journey. I will always gratefully remember them. Their thoughts and challenges have been gifts to me. Gustavo Gutiérrez remains a source of inspiration, insight, and support, and a much admired friend.

Philosopher Raúl Fornet-Betancourt has been an important conversation partner. Over many years, as professor of philosophy at Germany's University of Bremen and as a leader of the *Missio* Institute at Aachen, he has created an impressive intercultural philosophy that has very much impacted my own work and the work of many other scholars around the world. His thought is one of the great philosophical contributions over the past several decades, and one shaping much of my work. I am deeply grateful for his philosophical insights and for his life and friendship. Now I join him in retirement.

I also want to thank the Academy of Catholic Hispanic Theologians of the United States, the Hispanic Theological Initiative, the American Academy of Religion, *La Comunidad* of Hispanic Scholars in Religion, the Catholic Theological

Society of America, and the Hispanic Summer Program, for creating spaces that empower conversations, challenges, and consultations among scholars.

My sincere gratitude also goes to Robert Ellsberg and Orbis Books for the many years of trusting and publishing my work.

Those whose names appear on the dedicatory page at the start of this volume and in the preceding paragraphs have been conversation partners over the years, as have also Néstor Medina, Jesús M. Zaglul, C-Vanessa White, Edwin D. Aponte, M. Shawn Copeland, Peter Hünermann, María del Socorro Castañeda, Thomas Schreijäck, Elías Ortega, Efraín Agosto, Jamie T. Phelps, Sharon S. Ringe, Bryan Massingale, Jennifer Owens-Jofré, Robert J. Rivera, Jeremy V. Cruz, Allan Figueroa Deck, Maria Clara L. Bingemer, Paulo Fernando C. de Andrade, Cesar Kuzma, Ángel F. Méndez Montoya, Roberto C. Espinoza, Car. González y Rosario Padilla, Richard McCarron, Mayra Rivera R., Lauren Guerra A., Michael S. Campos, Michael Angell, Juan Oliver, Penelope Bridges and the community of St. Paul's Episcopal Cathedral in San Diego, Salvador Arce, Joanne Rodríguez and Angela Schoepf, Anthony Suárez, Nichole Flores, Izak Santana, Elaine Padilla, Ramón Luzárraga, Juan Hernández, Jacqueline Hidalgo, María Teresa Dávila, Rebecca Berrú-Davis, Hugo Córdova Q., Cláudio Carvalhaes, Daisy L. Machado, José R. Irizarry, Antonio E. Alonso, Neomi de Anda, Carmen Chávez, José David Rodríguez, Alberto L. García, Claire Collins, Luis A. Vera, Charles R. Lyndaker, Miguel G. Ramos, Jeff González, Rosa and Miguel Frías, Mari Castellanos, Alberto Embry, Rubén Moreno S., and Enrique Cortés.

Some friends, colleagues and teachers are no longer with us, as they now rest in peace. I want to acknowledge them

also, with gratitude: John J. Nevins, Virgilio Elizondo, Edgard
Beltrán, Robert Schreiter, Alejandro García-Rivera, Ada María
Isasi–Díaz, Juan M. Acosta, Juan M. Montalvo, Carlos J. Botta,
Eugenio Marcano, Julio Cicero, James V. Vitucci, Alan Beau-
regard, Kathleen Dugan, Jack Lindquist, Bernard Cooke,
Siegfried Wiedenhofer, Tomás Marín, Carlota Guerra, José de
Mesa, and Otto Maduro.

My most heartfelt gratitude is for Ricardo and both of
our families. Without Ricardo I would not have become the
human I am—nor the theologian. He has been inspiration,
foundation, *compañero y amigo*, for more than thirty years. His
decades of dedicated work on behalf of San Diego's vulnerable
can factually be described as admirable, indispensable, and
inspiring. His service to refugees seeking asylum on our local
border has also been and remains extraordinary. Ricardo's life
and work are a clear example of compassionate and effective
solidarity. He is courageously and unambiguously committed
to serve those most in need. Ricardo has kept my feet on the
ground and taught me to stay rooted in *lo cotidiano* of our
shared life and of our Latinoax communities. He is a sacrament
of God's presence in my life. As my late mother once told me,
"He made you human." Our families in Mexicali, Miami, and
Santo Domingo have been and remain sources of strength, of
growth, and of pride for both of us.

Thank you! *¡Gracias! Obrigado!*

Orlando O. Espín
San Diego, CA

Index

Sun
    and divinity, 86, 89–91, 110
    Nahua as People of the, 110
Supreme Originating God, 110
symbols
    and cultural context, 1, 5*n8*, 7, 30,
        132
    and empowerment, 58–60
    Marian, 69, 72–74, 115, 123
    Nahua, 74, 87*n35*, 89, 104*n57*,
        112–13
    and power asymmetries, 12, 31, 61,
        114
    reinterpreting, 70–71, 125–26, 133

Tenochtitlan, 81–86, 90, 109, 115, 117
Teotihuacan, 90
Tepanec, 83
Tepeyac
    chapel, 115–16, 119
    etymology, 115*n77*
    Guadalupan apparition, 75, 120
    and Luis Lasso de la Vega, 118
    and Nahua beliefs, 120
    opposition to new painting, 118
    opposition to worship, 116*n81*
    popularity, 117
Tepeyacac, 115
Testera, Jacobo de, 99*n48*
Testerian manuscripts, 99*n48*, 104
Tezcatlipoca, 88
theologizing subjects, 23–24
theology
    Caputo on, 53
    and Eurocentrism, xvii, 22–23, 129
    and interculturality, 25–26
    and Latinoax communities, xii, xviii
    and power asymmetries, xv, 5*n8*
    Russian Orthodox, 44*n57*
Thiselton, Anthony C., 37*n47*
Titizano, Cecilia, 66–67, 124*n91*
Tlacaclel, 85–86, 89*n37*
Tlaloc, 89–90
Tlaxcala, 85*n34*
Tlíllan Tlapállan, 90

Tlóque 'Nahuaque, 88, 110*n69*
Toltecs, 83, 85, 88–90
Tonantzin, 74, 89, 115*n78*. *See also*
        goddess figures
topoi, 26
traditioning, 5*n8*, 31*n40*, 37, 81–82,
        104*n58*
transience, xvi, 7, 21, 26–28, 30
Treaty of Guadalupe Hidalgo, 82*n31*
Trinitarian doctrine, 49*n65*, 91, 96–99,
        103, 105–6, 112
Trinitarian monotheism,
        57*n83*, 98–100
Trinity
    in art, 104–6, 111
    colonial teachings on, 57, 105
    Eurocentric views, 92, 96–97, 100,
        103, 135
    and gender, 73, 102
Trouillot, Michel-Rolph, 23*n30*
truth claims, 18–19, 37*n47*, 51

Ultimate Mystery, 102
UNESCO, 36*n46*
United States
    Catholicism in, xii, 34, 46*n61*, 67*n4*
    and Latinoax communities, xi–xii,
        33–34
    Southwest, xii, 33
    and theology, 24*n32*, 61
universality
    cultural, 21–22
    and validity, 18, 22

Valeriano, Antonio, 119–20
Vatican I, 13, 40–41
Vatican II, 35*n45*, 38*n49*, 40*n54*, 106*n62*
Virgen de Belén, xiii
Virgen de Fátima, xiii
Virgen de Guadalupe
    apparitions, 74–75, 81, 119–20
    author's works on, 65*n1*
    devotion, xiv–xv, 74–75, 77
    Extremaduran, 92, 115–18
    and goddess figures, 74

148

Index